SEASONS

Other Books by Hal Borland

An American Year
The Enduring Pattern
Beyond Your Doorstep
Sundial of the Seasons
Countryman: A Summary of Belief
Our Natural World (*Editor*)
Hill Country Harvest
Homeland: A Report from the Country
This Hill, This Valley
High, Wide and Lonesome
Country Editor's Boy
The Dog Who Came to Stay
Penny
The Seventh Winter
The Amulet
When the Legends Die
King of Squaw Mountain
Rocky Mountain Tipi Tales
The Youngest Shepherd
America Is Americans

Other Books by Les Line

Puffin Island
Mystery of the Everglades
What We Save Now (*Editor*)
The Sea Has Wings
Dining on a Sunbeam

SEASONS

by Hal Borland

Photographs
by Les Line

J.B. LIPPINCOTT COMPANY
Philadelphia and New York

Picture portfolios designed by Walter Miles

U.S. Library of Congress Cataloging in Publication Data

Borland, Hal Glen, birth date
    Seasons.
    1. Nature. I. Line, Les, illus. II. Title.
QH81.B754   500.9   73-5988
ISBN-0-397-00996-8

Some parts of this text first appeared in *Audubon* and in *The Progressive*. I thank Les Line, editor of *Audubon*, and Morris H. Rubin, editor of *The Progressive*, for agreeing to the use of that material in this form. The greater part of the text has never before been in print.

H. B.

For Barbara and for Lois

Foreword

There are two basic dimensions for this remarkable planet we call Earth—time and distance. Both are fantastic variables. Distance is the space between two spinning atoms, the length of a man's arm, the span of a continent, the reach of a man's imagination. Time is the moon's phases, the interval of an ice age, the duration of a sleepless night, the pause between two throbs of my own pulse.

With all our clocks and our measuring sticks, the most we can do is divide some of the more common aspects of time and distance into manageable fragments. Yet it is within these two dimensions that most of our lives are lived.

Here, in these essays, I have somewhat simplified those boundaries in one sense, expanded them in another. Time here is primarily a matter of days, bounded by sunrises, and seasons, which are without fixed perimeters but which inevitably add up to years. But distance here is the reach of the human eye and hand, the scope of understanding. It is the reach to the bluet in the May meadow, the effort to under-stand the snowflake's sixfold mystery; the reach to the summer horizon, the effort to comprehend the January sky, the sun, the moon, the lodestar around which swing the constellations.

Essentially, we are concerned here with the wonder of life as we know it on Earth, the only form of life that we know beyond any doubt does exist. And a year, one of Earth's circuits around the sun, is the pattern I have chosen, one year, four seasons. It is possible, even probable, that the forms of life we know were fostered by and are eternally dependent on that rhythm, which can be simply stated as sprouting, growth, ripening, and rest. Or, in the terms we more often use, spring, summer, autumn, and winter.

But if we go too far along that track, reducing the wonders to numbers and chemical formulas, we begin to dissect those wonders, to analyze protoplasm and count chromosomes. That is all very well in the laboratory, where the physicists and the chemists try to get at the secrets that will explain life, at least in their terms. But a distinction persists between life and its components that adds up to the wonder and makes this such a remarkable world. A tree, for instance, is more than so many planks and so much sawdust, so many rolls of paper and so many gallons of turpentine. You can dissect a tree and get those components, as well as various others. But nobody yet has found a way to create a tree from planks, sawdust, paper, and turpentine. We still have to start with a seed and grow it, slowly, season by season, year by year, to get a tree.

That is what I mean by the wonder, which defies laboratories. And that is what this book is about: Four seasons, which we call spring, summer, autumn or fall, and winter. It is about the look, the smell, the taste, the feel, and whole sense of life in the natural world around us. It is about the wonder of that life, the marvel of it and the glory.

Almost every day someone tells me there is very little natural world left. What these people mean, of course, is that not much of that natural world is visible from where they stand, in the midst of a crowd, or that they are so absorbed by thruway traffic or fly so high and so fast that they don't see what they are passing as they are zoomed from one metropolis to another. But there still is a natural world out there beyond the urban sprawl. Too many of its streams, too much of its soil, too much of its air, are polluted, thanks to an economy of waste and heedless extrava-

gance. But the fact is that over much of this country streams still flow from the uplands to the sea, grass and trees still grow in meadow and woodland, birds sing and mate and nest, insects hum and buzz and leave their hostages to tomorrow in egg and pupae. Out there, I can testify as a lifelong witness, sunsets and moonrises mark the nights and sunrises and open skies mark the days.

Make no mistake about it, this country is not all concrete and steel and glass, not all high-rise apartments, beehive offices, roaring factories. It merely seems so from the canyons of those metropolitan centers where more than 70 percent of the people live. But all those urbanites occupy less than 2 percent of the land in these United States. That leaves a great many hills and valleys to the trees and grass.

If all the land in this country were evenly divided among all the people, there would be almost ten acres apiece, about five average city blocks for each man, woman, and child. If all the people in this country were somehow gathered in New York State, there would be a 50-by-75-foot lot for each of them—and all the other forty-eight contiguous continental states would be unoccupied land.

So when these essays discuss the open countryside and the natural life there, they are not talking about a never-never land or something that vanished a hundred years ago. This world of spring peepers and buds, of summer blossoms and nesting birds, of autumn harvest and vivid woodlands, of winter's sharp air and deep, dark cold, is as real as daylight and as persistent as time itself. It is the world from which we grew, as a race, as a species. It is the home, the source, the reassurance when we relax our human arrogance enough to ask ourselves who and what we are, and why, and when we have the courage to face the answers.

These essays, then, are one countryman's findings, his personal report. They are dispatches from the open country, seasonal reports in the oldest continuing story known to man, the story of life on earth. I haven't really covered this story, of course; nobody ever will. But I have been setting down progress reports for some years, in books, essays, and editorials, and this book is another installment of those reports. That is my purpose. That is why I have spent so much time interviewing trees, in a manner of speaking, investigating swamps and woodlands, attending conventions of crows and grackles, gathering statistics from milkweed pods, goldenrod flowers and snowflakes, being on hand for sunrises, thunderstorms, and Harvest Moons.

Fortunately, Les Line, editor of *Audubon* magazine and one of the foremost outdoor photographers I know, as well as a distinguished naturalist, has perfectly complemented my text with his pictures. His photography has added a further dimension to this book, given it visual proportions that words alone could not achieve.

Here, then, are these dispatches, verbal and pictorial, from the American countryside. They are current, not ultimate in any sense, current installments in a story that I hope will continue for many more millennia.

H. B.

Salisbury, Conn.
1973

SEASONS

(Page 12)
Snow melts, ice thaws, brooks flow free again.
The voice of spring is heard in running water,
and its face is seen in bright reflections.

Spring

I will be seeing the first red-winged blackbirds any day now, and will hear them chattering in the leafless trees at the edge of the little bog down the road where I saw skunk cabbage poking its purple-green hoods up through the ice a month ago. When the redwings arrive I can begin to watch for pussy willows, those tiny wild ones. They will appear in silvery coats of fur, and in another two or three weeks they will mature into blossoms. The first blackbirds will be the males, with those red epaulettes—some of the red, as a matter of fact, faded to a yellowish white. The females, which look so much like big sparrows they often go unidentified, lag behind the males ten days or so. But by the time they get here the hylas, the spring peepers, will certainly be out and yelping. And the migrant robins, which should arrive this week, will be all over our pastures, chattering among themselves but not yet singing. They won't sing much for two weeks or so, until they get settled here in the valley, but after that they will waken me before sunrise.

It is winter ending, spring beginning, a reiteration of the oldest statement we know, but a reiteration with infinite variations. Spring is land emerging from water, ice retreating from lowlands, amphibians emerging from the mud of hibernation, leaves bursting from buds, birds returning from the tropics, the silence of winter ending in birdsong, beehum, chirp, chitter, and all the variations of the mating call.

If I had been skeptical or really curious about when spring was going to arrive here in the lower Berkshires, I could have watched the isotherms on the weather maps. Spring travels north, for all practical purposes, with the 35-degree isotherm. Or I might have charted the afternoon temperature here and forecast the appearance of the peepers. They come out of the mud and start yelping for mates when the temperature gets up to 50 and stays there at least three days in a row. If it dives into the teens, of course, they go back into the mud for a few days; but I have heard them out and yelping loudly in the midst of an early April snowstorm, really an uncanny experience.

Some things, however, need no documentation, and spring is one of them. If I didn't believe in spring I would have to wipe the slate clean and say I didn't believe in life. And I don't see how anybody could do that in late March or early April. In December, maybe, or even in February. But certainly not now. Not if you are aware of this world of reality.

Not long ago I read a complaint about critics of urban life by a man who was so insular that he was almost incredible. Yet he said, "There is an abiding sense of isolation and anachronism about rural life and rural people," and he went on to proclaim that in the city "spring occurs every time there's a new museum exhibit or hit show or pennant race. The seasons of the mind," he persisted, "do not wait upon the equinox—the bloom of a new fashion and the eclipse of a celebrity's glow are small parts of a man-made world spinning far faster than the leisurely pace of our planet." And so on, through as myopic a demonstration of imperception as I have read in a long time.

There was a man who had no conception of reality, who thought he spun the world and set the time for sunrise. There spake the man who once said, just before the barbarians took over, that Rome would live forever, the man who stood in the streets of Pompeii and told his companions that Etna never would erupt again.

Spring, as anyone with eyes in his head and two grains of understanding knows instinctively, is far more than the blooming of a new fashion. It is ooze and wetlands, melt and seep and watery margins. It recapitulates the remote past, before the arrogance of humanity was even dreamed of; when dry land was something new and amphibian life was in its first stages of learning to live there. Once it learned that tremendous lesson, it populated the land with hordes that are incredible today. Even the much later hordes that lived at the foot of the retreating ice sheets must have been stupendous, for there was an urgency about life in that geological springtime that we can scarcely comprehend today.

I think, when March ends, of spring as I knew it in my own early springtime, when I, too, was young and lived on the High Plains of Colorado. Melt from the winter's snow was everywhere. Vast lagoons spread over the shallowest of hollows on the uplands, acres broad and inches deep. There the green of spring fringed the shallow water and burgeoned under it as under a greenhouse roof— buffalo grass, grama grass, upland bluestem, all warmed by the sun and watered by the melt, all growing like mad.

In those vast lagoons and all around them were migrant waterfowl, the aquatic birds of the whole West and Southwest. Everything, it sometimes seemed, except pelicans. I never saw a pelican there, but there were upland plover, killdeer, brant,

Canada geese and snow geese, ducks of a dozen species, snipe, long-billed curlews, rails, gallinules, spotted sandpipers— name them, they were there, birds we plainsmen wouldn't see again till next spring's melt again made the uplands a vast wading pool for herons. I saw great blues there, which we called shitepokes, and green herons for which we had no names. There was an occasional bittern, hunched-shouldered and source of those sounds so like the sound of someone driving a stake into the ground. Frogs trilled. Toads shrilled. Meadowlarks and horned larks and lark buntings fluttered and sang, but they were natives and went almost unnoticed while those vernal flocks of exotic aliens were there.

Then the migrants moved on, in vast flurries of wings and with loud honking and quacking and chattering. The pools dried up, leaving only the grass and the wild onions and the resinweed and the little red mallows we called cowboy's delight. And only in the buffalo wallows and the deep-hollow waterholes was there enough water to hatch tadpoles and mosquito wigglers. There were new pups in the prairie-dog towns, and newly hatched burrowing owls that looked like wads of gray lint. The wheatgrass and the valley bluestem quickly got their growth, pushed by snow melt and April rain. Then it was June and summer.

There was no such teeming rush the first spring we spent in these lower Berkshires, twenty-odd years ago. Geese came over, arrowing north, great skeins of them with their high-distant gabbling. Ducks came in flocks, mostly blacks and mallards, and found nesting places on the banks of ponds and in brush along the river, even while the ice was still on the lakes. Peepers made their shrill clamor, frogs trilled, and all the migrant birds came back and saluted the mornings with a great jubilee of song. But there was no quick, warm rush of birth and reawakening. Nights stayed chilly, and days were cool with only an occasional hot afternoon. Impatient, I asked an old-timer if we weren't ever going to have spring, and he said with a smile, "We had spring last Thursday. Didn't you notice?" Even the greening of the pasture grass and the leafing of the maples was a gradual process. Spring crept in, on wary, hesitant feet.

But now I know what to expect. When I see and hear the redwings I don't think I will wake up tomorrow to a teeming world of sudden vernal achievement. April here is a time of slow preparation. If I seek them out, I can find hepaticas in bloom. On a warm south slope I may find even a few brave anemones in flower. Up on the ledges, where the rocks catch the sun's warmth, wild columbines are now beginning to thrust their first blue-green rosettes of leaves through the pockets of leaf mold. On the warm side of an old stone wall I can find jacks-in-the-pulpit coming up like slim, green lance points, and nearby will be the first, furled leaves of bloodroot.

But this is not exactly teeming spring. It is gradual, leisurely spring, and it reminds me of the gradual springtime of life on this planet. If it achieves a handful of violets by May Day it will pretty well have kept to its usual schedule. May is the time when our spring achieves its real bounty, its lilacs and apple blossoms and columbines and wild geraniums. By late April there will be promises everywhere, and the human heart that knows the difference between a museum exhibit and a rural hillside can begin to sing with the robins and the orioles in the morning. But for real accomplishment we have to wait, with the bees, for May's florescence. By May everything from pine trees to bluets will be in full bloom.

I have spoken of the springtime of life, of all life. Even to speculate about that, we must think in eons, not in seasons or years or even in centuries.

That springtime began in what the geologists call the Archeozoic Era, a billion and a half years ago. Yes, that is one thousand five hundred million years ago, fifteen million centuries ago. At that time the earth was largely if not entirely covered by oceans whose waters were warmed by volcanic action. In those warm waters, life somehow originated. There are various theories and speculations about its beginnings, none of which can be proved and none of which wholly explain how it happened. But the fact remains that the first germs of life appeared, flecks of single-celled life capable of reproducing themselves.

Liken those first protozoans to the earliest buds of spring, which have in them tremendous potentialities. Or to the seeds in the soil as the strengthening sunlight of early March begins to warm the earth. A week passes, in our terms of time, a few hundred million years in geologic terms. Little change is evident. A few more weeks, and those protozoans, those buds and seeds of life, have begun to produce strange offspring, creatures that are multicellular. Now the first of the corals and sponges and marine worms can be seen in least in embryo.

A month passes, in earth time, a billion years in geologic time. We call it April. In geologic terms it is the Paleozoic Era, the Cambrian Period. There are lowland areas now, land that emerged from the seas only a few million years ago. In the oceans are teeming hordes of strange creatures, none of them with backbones. But the seeds have sprouted, the buds have begun to open.

Another week—time is passing swiftly now, and even in geologic terms it is only a few hundred million years—and there is plant life on land, in the tepid shallows, primitive plants seeking to find and hold a place there. And in the oceans there are sharks, bony fishes, mollusks. Out of the ocean's life, too, have evolved in some totally miraculous and unknown way the first air-breathing creatures. Spiders and scorpions have sprung from one of those obscure buds that we first knew as protozoans.

Less than another week, less than a hundred million years, and there is a rush of opening buds of life. Now there are huge tree ferns on land, and the vegetation has begun to claim all the lowlands, jungles of plants. The first fish have come ashore and learned to breathe the open air, and they have become the first amphibians. The first primitive reptiles are foraging through those fern-tree jungles which, in the course of time, will become today's coal beds. And in the air are swarms and clouds of insects, ants, bees, flies, midges, and a number of insect giants, dragonflies with two-foot wingspreads, cockroaches two inches long. The age of giantism is at hand.

Then it is mid-May, less than two hundred million years ago, and the giant reptiles rule the land, the ichthyosaurs, the phytosaurs, the dinosaurs, and the pterodactyls, the first animals that achieved anything like flight.

And as the days pass, those long geological days, and we come to the Cretaceous Period, less than a hundred and fifty million years ago, the continents have largely assumed the form we know, the Rocky Mountains and the Andes are rising, and the giant reptiles are about to vanish. The mammals, which were mere rat-sized fugitives in the underbrush fifty million years before, now begin to outnumber the reptiles. They have become the dominant tribe of the earth, they and the birds and

the insects. And on the dry land there are flowering plants for the first time.

It is June, late spring, and geologically we are up within a hundred million years or so of the present. Those seeds and buds that we knew as protozoans back in early March of this geological calendar have sprouted and grown and opened into a vast multitude of life forms. And not the least of them is man. Nor is the least of them, for that matter, the violet or the buttercup or the mourning cloak butterfly or the ephemeral Mayfly. Whatever may be the reason and the meaning of life, we partake, all of us, and we respond in some way to that resurgence we know as springtime.

I have known a great variety of springs since that springtime of my life on the High Plains of the West. I have known March and April in the Carolinas, where the robins and their migrant kinfolk barely pause on their way northward, with that 35-degree isotherm. I have known the springtime of laurel in the Great Smokies, when whole mountainsides seemed to be in blossom at once. I have known the plains of Texas in bluebonnet time, when it seemed the whole countryside, the whole vast span of rangeland, was carpeted with those beautiful lupines. I have known Maine slowly emerging from its deep refrigeration, a land of pine woods and rocky coasts and April melt and May blossom, flowers thrice welcome for their late arrival. I have known the marshes and wetlands of Minnesota and northern Dakota when April began to open their waters and the incredible flocks of ducks and geese came streaming in, pouring up that great midland flyway with all the urgency of spring itself, the irresistible force of life driven toward the nesting grounds, toward reproduction.

One April we went down the Shenandoah Valley. It was late April and a mild season, and all day we drove through a vast garden of apple blossoms. We traveled slowly, stopping often to smell the air, to hear the hum of God only knows how many bees, to see the slight, subtle variations and combinations of pink and shimmering white that marked one orchard from another.

We came home to a spell of raw, chilly weather, the kind that so often casts a shadow over May in New England. Our own apple trees were in fat bud, but they simply sat there and waited. Then came the turn, also characteristic of New England, and all the warmth of spring descended on us like a summer rain. Within twenty-four hours our apple trees came into flower, all their buds' pent-up energy released in one pink and white burst. With eight big old apple trees in the backyard and along the pasture fence, it was like living in the midst of a vast bouquet. Also, from midmorning till late afternoon, it was like living in a beehive. Every tree was alive with honeybees. When I stood under a tree and looked up it seemed that every blossom had its bee and the whole tree shimmered with those tiny wings. The hum was a day-long drone that we could hear even inside the house.

The honeybees always have a field day when those apple trees bloom, but I was surprised one evening when I went out at eight o'clock and heard an even louder hum. The honeybees should have been through for the day, I thought. They were, in fact. This hum came from bumblebees. The big old snow-apple tree that overhangs the woodshed was alive with them.

This was a new one to me. I went to another tree and another, and found six trees alive with the big bees, not as many as honeybees at midday, but literally hundreds of them. And the buzz they made was twice as loud as that of the honeybees.

What had happened was that another facet of spring had just revealed itself, perhaps by coincidence. The first annual hatch of bumblebees had come out only a few days before, and they were full of hunger-driven energy. Had the apples bloomed a week earlier, not been held back by that cold spell, the honeybees would have pretty well completed the harvest before the bumblebees got a chance at it. But here came the bumblers, and they found those fresh apple blossoms. *Eureka!*

They were all small bumblebees, only about two thirds as big as the midsummer bumblers. And they were twice as busy as the big bumblebees that loaf around the clover heads in June. And that itself proved the point.

Bumblebees have a different life cycle from honeybees. Young bumblebee queens mate in early autumn, then hibernate, usually in such an underground haven as a deserted mouse nest. Those queens are the only bumblebees that survive the winter. Spring comes and the fertile queens awaken and set up housekeeping, each by herself, in hollows and holes in the soil. There each queen builds an egg cell, stocks it with pollen and nectar from the earliest spring flowers—crocuses are among their favorites—then lays a clutch of eggs and closes the cell. Then she makes a rather crude wax honey jug, no bigger than her own body, and fills it with thin honey, a kind of rainy-day pantry she can use in bad weather.

In a late spring she may have a hard time finding enough flowers to stock the egg cell with pollen and nectar, and she may have hungry days herself. But she guards the eggs and makes out. The eggs hatch into larvae that feed on the nectar and pollen in their cell, supplemented by special meals the queen-mother brings from time to time. The larvae reach full growth in ten days, then make thin, papery cocoons in which they pupate for a week or two. Finally they emerge as mature bumblebees, the first members of the new colony. They are undersized, they are all sterile females, and they have a compulsion to work.

With these workers, the queen can live a less strenuous life. They feed her, lay up a small store of honey for emergencies

such as several days of cold, wet weather. The queen lays more eggs and the workers tend them, feed the larvae far better than the queen fed the first brood, and take care of the pupae. The next hatch is bigger. Thus the colony grows, and thus the bumblebees become full-sized. By late summer a few fertile females are hatched from special eggs, and a hatch of males appears. Those females will mate and become the young queens who will hibernate, full of fertile eggs for the following spring, when the cycle starts all over again.

The bumblebees make only a limited amount of honey, just enough for emergency food for the current season. Most of the big ones we see after late June are males, rather lazy fellows who fend for themselves and do no work for the colony. The big ones we see early, in April and early May, are the young queens, gathering pollen and nectar to feed those first broods. Those I saw in our apple trees were members of the first brood from several colonies, brought to hatch by the warm spell after being held back, as the apple blossoms were, by the earlier raw, chilly weather.

Man planted those apple orchards in the Shenandoah Valley, and those here on our farm, and tended and cared for them. But, especially in the spring, I am convinced that man really had nothing to do with the blossoming of those trees, no matter how he hybridized and selected and grafted in his nurseries. And I know he had nothing to do, really, with their fruiting, which is so largely a consequence of the bees. Flowers have bloomed, seeds and fruit have been borne, the plants and their produce have matured and new plants have sprouted and grown, for a long, long time. This began before there was such a creature as man on earth, and it will continue after he is gone. The more springs I experience, the more certain I am that man may huff and puff, storm and demand, and not change by one microsecond the timetable of spring or alter in the slightest any detail of spring's achievement. Man has enough trouble getting along with himself and his own kind. If he would only pause and see how absurd is his dream of omnipotence, the earth would be better off, and I suspect that man would, too.

Actually, spring invites participation, even though it does not need human help. Sap rises in the trees, and human beings who are not urbanized beyond redemption feel something like the urgencies of sap-rise in themselves. Spring brings its own renewal after the winter of attrition. We are not exactly as the grass, but when the green comes again to the pastures and the lawns, we too are renewed. Brooks flow freely again. The squirrels are capering. There is something in the very air, out beyond the pall of smog, that seems to say anything is possible.

One reason we react as we do is that there is chlorophyll in our blood. And that's not wholly a figure of speech. The hemoglobin in my blood, the chemists tell me, is chemically closely akin to the chlorophyll in a leaf. The difference, substantially, is only an atom or two of iron. I suspect that plants and birds and animals and people have something of the same reaction. It would be amazing if they don't, for we are all a part of that mysterious, universal stream we call life.

The sap rises, usually in March and April here in my corner of the country, and the trees begin to respond. And what I have just called the sap-rise occurs in me soon after. I am doubly aware of the urgencies of spring around me. I even see the showers of bud scales.

Bud scales are so inconspicuous that we seldom notice them, yet there they are, covering and protecting the infant leaf or blossom all winter. Then comes the first warmth of spring and the buds respond. They begin to grow, and like children they outgrow their clothes. At a certain point, determined by the temperature and the sun's angle, the wax that has sealed the bud scales melts, the scales are pushed back, the leaf or flower pokes its nose out for the first time. And the bud scales loosen and fall.

On most trees those bud scales are some shade of brown. They seldom are more than a quarter of an inch long, though on trees of the hickory family they are far larger and run to shades of tan and pink, quite spectacular when the fantastic hickory buds open. As the buds become leaves or blossoms, there is a rain of bud scales in the woodland. In villages with trees, particularly with elms, along the streets, you will often find windrows of those brown scales in the gutters in May. In the woodland they are largely lost in the usual woodland litter, but there they are, literally billions of them, even more than there are leaves falling in October.

This rain of bud scales is another example of how the trees indulge in what looks like extravagance but actually is strict economy. Trees use their own discard, in the form of leaf mold and mulch. It isn't waste at all, but a kind of endless process by which the plant world thrives on its own litter. And bud scales are only one item in what might be called the springtime compost heap of the woodland.

Just up the road from our house is a huge old cottonwood. When its buds open it sheds literally pecks of bud scales, each scale big as one of my fingernails. Then the long, reddish-brown catkins appear, scatter their pollen, and begin to fall. For a time the ground and the road beneath that tree are covered with those catkins, like big, fat, reddish-brown caterpillars. This is one of the most spectacular blossom falls I know, another item in building that natural compost heap. But the maples do the same thing. I see it most plainly under the red maples. As their stamens complete their pollen function, they fall, small tassels of long-stemmed stamens, red and eye-catching. Where those maples overhang the road

there is a blood-red stain big as the tree's diameter, a stamen stain, for a week or ten days each year.

Another form of throwaway, or profligacy, is in the pollen from the trees, particularly from the conifers, which scatter it in incredible quantity. The big Norway spruce here beside our house makes the air shimmer when its male blossoms open. The golden-yellow pollen dusts and lightly colors the grass beneath it. And that pollen drifts onto our front porch in unbelievable quantities. One year I swept up almost half a pint of it from the porch. When you remember that those pollen grains are dust-fine, so small they will drift in the air, you may realize the incredible number of individual grains there must be in half a pint of them. I am sure we haven't the numbers, at least in conventional mathematics, to count them. But that pollen, too, goes to help make the compost that feeds the roots of the trees.

Perhaps another example, taken from the springtime of life I was speaking of a few paragraphs back, will emphasize this point. In the days of the tree-fern forests, trees and virtually all plant life reproduced by spores. This was before plants had evolved to the point of flowering and producing fertile seeds. The spores of those tree ferns were as fine as the pollen of my Norway spruce. Yet there were so many of those trees and they produced so many spores that the cannel coal and the jet that are mined today were formed of those ancient spore beds. The spores sifted down from the trees in quantities that I cannot even imagine, formed layers many feet thick, and later were pressed and concentrated into those hard, black, rocklike substances we mine today.

That was in the geologic spring of life, and the showering of pollen that replaces the rain of spores still goes on, the pollen and the blossoms and the bud scales. The eons pass, and the turn of the earth doesn't even falter. Now it heaves over slowly, as it has for untold millennia, and we in the Northern Hemisphere face the sun more directly. All things are believable again, all things that matter, all the strange and wonderful ways of life. Including such minor matters as crocus blossoms and anemones and hepatica, such major matters as maple trees and oaks with new leaves all through the woodland. There is a newness, a remaking of remembered detail, and a reshaping of hilltop and meadowland.

And in all of us there is a newness and the oldness renewed.

Granted, spring doesn't put an end to wars or want or bias or greed or envy. It doesn't exorcise devils or sanctify the actions of rogues. It does little to improve the cities and other urban concentrations that look with scorn upon direct contact with the earth, the rootbed of life. But it does make life worth living, if you know what it is and where to find it.

Maybe the first full moon of spring is just another full moon, but that is debatable. Maybe the stars, now in their springtime places, are the same stars that have been there to see since man first looked up and saw a star, but what is more wonderful than a spring evening, with that whole sense of life stirring underfoot and the air alive with starlight?

Maybe the old apple trees in my backyard are the same trees, spared when the big orchard was cut by a previous owner before I came here because that man liked to make his own cider, but when those trees burst bud and appear in full blossom they are new as sunrise—and old as time. And that's another thing about spring: it brings the half-forgotten back for a remembering, and the longer one lives the more springs have been half forgotten.

Oh, I can sing all the praises I wish, but the real songs of spring are sung by the robin and the oriole and the tanager.

The trees, we sometimes say, aren't aware how the earth and stars line up for the vernal equinox. They can't calculate such matters. But when all is said and done, anyone can chart an equinox, if he tries and if it is really important to him. But it takes a seed to perpetuate life. Give a seed a place to grow, light and warmth to inspire it—give it spring—and anything can happen. I know that, deep down in my viscera, even more firmly than in my brain. I know that a seed is somehow aware of an equinox without so much as setting down one figure, aware even of a sunny day in April. On second thought,

I am not even sure that my knowledge is intellectual at all. It is as instinctive in me as it is in a seed, and it comes to the surface now and then, especially in the spring. Especially when I see bluets in bloom, or Dutchman's-breeches, or marsh marigolds. I know that if a bluet can happen, anything can happen.

And that is spring, that thought, that belief. The equinox is merely a figure on a chart, something that accompanies change and gives it a point of reference. But spring is the beginning of things so new, so pristine, so absolutely fresh from the source that they have the very look of Genesis.

Spring *is* Genesis, year after year. That's the sum of it.

The prairie chicken cock, Western cousin of
the East's ruffed grouse, struts, cackles, clucks,
and booms in his springtime courtship dance.

Spring...
A Portfolio

Each year's spring is the ending of another miniature Ice Age. Winter's
darkness thins away. Ice that choked lakes and streams begins to break up.
The sun, too long a far-off, reluctant glow, at last warms the daytime air. Hill-
sides are alive with melt—trickling water from shadowed snowbanks in the
woods, creeping toward brook and river, toward the mother sea. Frost oozes
from the ground. Roots waken from deep sleep, quickening with a new span
of daylight. Sap rises in the maple. Buds fatten on the willow. Hepatica thrusts
leaf and lavender petal up through moldering litter. Spring peepers quit
muddy hibernation to trill vernal mating calls. Robins return from the
South. The whole repletion of sprouting and growth, flowering and fruiting,
ripeness and renewal, is under way again, the purpose of life, the reason for
being. The Earth rouses. The great rhythm throbs with the pulse of re-creation
after the long, cold sleep.

Skunk cabbage, hooded granther of the bogs, melts its way up
through the ice of March by "running a fever" as high as 27 degrees
above the surrounding air. Its spadix of fetid little flowers
attracts carrion flies, and it is through blooming before
sweet flowers of April come to bud, in leaf before the trees.

Threefold in leaf and petal,
the trilliums start in April
with deep-red wake-robins.
In May come the painted ones,
white with crimson markings.
Then the large-flowered whites,
most beautiful trilliums of all.
Those who pluck wake-robins
seldom pluck them twice—
they have a carrion odor.
Another common name for
them is stinking Benjamin.

Gold—that is spring's favorite color:
the marsh marigold's buttercup-yellow,
the creamy yellow of wild oats,
the deep golden yellow of trout lilies;
they bring the glow of sunlight
to the cool shadows of the woodland.

The Canada goose is the most famous traveler of our skies.
Who has not yearned to go with the gabbling skein arrowing
southward in November? Who has not greeted the returning flock,
even with snow in the air in March, as proof that spring is here?
They come back, explore the familiar places, and like any weary
traveler, luxuriate in a bath before they settle down to stay.
Then they begin to look for nesting places to raise a new generation.

*Geese mate for life, but it is mother goose who chooses
the site for a nest, builds it, and lays and hatches the eggs.
Father goose, belligerent as a bear, stands guard and drives off
any invader, man or beast—or tries to. When the young
are hatched he is fussy as a mother hen. But it is mother goose
who takes her fuzzy goslings for their first swim. With luck,
half of them will survive the summer and fly south come fall.*

Lady's slippers, we call them, and the botanical name means
Venus's buskins. They are the largest of our native orchids.
The yellow one grows two feet tall, often stands alone.
The pink one, the moccasin flower, has only two leaves,
and it often grows in large colonies in woodland shade.

Fiddleheads originated with ferns, not with violins. Like this cinnamon fern still fuzzed with infancy. By late May it will be a tall, graceful frond. The evergreen Christmas fern sends up new fronds every spring about the time the maples leaf out.

New leaves are delicate
as damselfly wings.
Ribs of young beech leaves
are like ribs in an X ray.
The Mayapple's umbrella
still shows its folds.
And a seedling oak, deep
in the woods, hangs leaves
like diapers to dry
in the spring sunlight.
Perhaps no more than 5
of 100 seedlings survive.

We have a dozen native dogwoods, tree, shrub, and herb, and their
bark once eased malaria and fortified a tonic. All greet spring
in a special way. Red osier's stems shine blood-red. The cornels
display flat-topped clusters of small white flowers.
Queen of them all is the flowering dogwood, Cornus florida.
To see its big white blossoms, like clouds of white butterflies
in the woods, is to have the best of all springtime tonics.

Summer

Summer is achievement, attainment of a purpose. The purpose is growth, life that achieves abundance and assures its own perpetuation. Summer doesn't wait for the solstice, in our latitude. It is rooted in the earth, not the almanac, and it comes when the leafy spread of chlorophyll has reached its maximum. Spring is opening buds and unfolding leaves, and summer comes when those leaves are fully spread to catch the long days of maximum sunlight. In the year's plan there is relatively little time for intense photosynthesis, the unique achievement of the green leaf; only a few months, and into that span must be compressed the whole year's growth as well as fruiting and seeding. There is no time to wait for a solstice, which is only the year's meridian, in any case, not in any sense a resting place or a pause in the year's occupation.

Summer comes in June, where I live, sometimes with June's first week. I don't have to see it coming. I hear it, in the dawn chorus of the birds, in the sibilance of the first cicadas in the warm afternoon, in the trilling of the frogs at late dusk. I smell it in the fragrance of new-cut hay drying in the sun, first cutting, first week in June. I feel it, in morning dew, in midday heat, in full-leaf shade in the woodland.

Maybe some can describe summer without first celebrating the end of May and the first of June. I can't.

By the last week in May the green world has begun to catch up with itself. I am always amazed at the way things happen, once the season is really committed, once spring has made the turn toward summer. We have three or four warm days in a row, then a July-hot day. The birches pop into leaf. The aspens flutter a day or two with fine silvery leaflets, then are full of bright green leaves, full-blown. The maples, which had leaves no bigger than a squirrel's ear ten days ago, suddenly are in full leaf, and there are great patches of shade where only last week there was sunlight. Apple blossoms fade and the lilacs pass their peak. Peonies are in fat bud.

That is May's end, June's beginning, the start of summer.

Some time in June's first week I waken and am up before five. A whole chorus of birdsong is in progress. A whippoorwill is reiterating his calls, for some mysterious reason, but he only makes the songsters sound more musical. As nearly as I can sort them out, there are robins, Baltimore orioles, scarlet tanagers, possibly a rose-breasted grosbeak, a couple of brown thrashers, and several I can't identify.

I have a cup of coffee, pull on a windbreaker and go out to feel the morning, see it, hear it. This is the time of year when every sense a man possesses gets a workout. You don't merely see this world; you participate in it.

I go down to the riverbank, see that the river is faintly steaming, the thin mist eddying in the air currents and lying only a few feet above the water. The grass is dripping with dew, the trunks of the maples black with moisture. Somewhere out on the water a fish leaps and splashes, probably a rock bass, maybe a yellow perch, maybe a German carp. Fifteen years ago it would have been a largemouth bass or a brown trout, and I would have had a boat at the dock and would have gone out for an hour of sunrise fishing. Now the pollution from upstream has driven out the trout and black bass, all the good fish. We keep hoping that some day the pollution laws will be enforced up there and the river will be brought back to life. Meanwhile, it is a beautiful river

to look at, and to remember as it used to be.

I walk down the road a way, to the middle pasture, and by now the light is bright enough that I can see the individual trees on the mountainside, though the top of the hill is still misted in. Out in the pasture I hear a snort and turn to look and see three deer, all does, standing only fifty yards away, watching me. I stop and they turn, flaunt their white flag-tails at me and lope off a little way, then pause and look at me again. They are cautious, but not really alarmed. I stand beside the fence and they watch me warily for a few minutes; then, deciding it is time to go, they float over the far fence and vanish into the brush on the hillside. Two of them were heavy with fawn, probably will drop their fawns within another two weeks.

I start on down the road, and a red-winged blackbird sees me, makes quite a fuss from a roadside tree. Probably his mate—or one of his mates, since redwings are polygamous—has a nest in the reeds on the riverbank nearby. Then a blue jay, the loudmouth of birddom, announces to the world that A Man is in sight. It doesn't seem to matter to the robins and orioles, who go right on singing.

A cottontail scurries from a tuft of roadside clover and vanishes in the pasture grass, which has shot up an inch a day the past two weeks. I stand for a few minutes watching the far side of the pasture strip, hoping to catch a glimpse of the red fox that has a den there. He sometimes hunts field mice in that area in the early morning. Once he came across the pasture and hunted mice just below the vegetable garden, not fifty yards from the house, at 8:30 in the morning. We watched from the kitchen window while he caught a mouse, toyed with it for five minutes before he ate it. But he is nowhere in sight this morning.

There's a woodchuck den hardly fifty feet from the fox den, but the chuck who lives there is seldom out for breakfast before sunrise. If I were a woodchuck I think I would sell that den, or even give it away, and move to some other neighborhood. But maybe that chuck thinks he is smarter than a fox. Maybe he is, at that. Or maybe he is just lucky. He's still alive.

I turn and come back toward the house, listening to the rush of Millstone Brook where it comes down a small rapid and spills out across the pasture. I am still small boy enough to think that someday I would like to whittle out a toy paddle wheel and set it in that brook and watch it turn.

Before I reach home the bird chorus has tapered off. Only a distant jay has to proclaim his existence, and even he relapses into silence after a few cries. I have never found the reason for that pause just before sunup. Only the light breeze rustles in the treetops and the brook keeps on its quiet murmuring. Just as I reach the front porch the first rays of the sun dazzle my eyes. It bounces over the horizon like a ball of silvery fire. And suddenly all the birds are singing again, twice as loud as before, it seems. The river mist is silvery and glinting, the dew on the grass gleams, and the maple leaves are all ashimmer. It is a brand-new day, June, and exultant with song.

That is the way June begins, for me at least. And by mid-June, no matter what year it is, we have reached a summary of all the Junes that ever were. June is a remembering, a knowing, a recalling of a time that was and is and always will be, a timeless time. Daisies whiten the roadsides, and they are remembered daisies. The bird songs are all songs that have been sung in human hearts since hearts first sang. Mid-June is hoped-for truth and longed-for beauty and dreamed-of happiness. It is hopes and longings and dreams that could come true five minutes from now.

Wild strawberries ripen, remembered perfection with the taste of yesterday's youth. Pasture roses bloom with the simplicity of beauty as new as the night's dew and as old as time itself. The sun approaches the meridian and there are more than fifteen hours of daylight. Shade lies cool and deep beneath the long-known maples. Fireflies wink in the lingering dusk, reminders of the long dusks of youth when fireflies were like starlight on the quiet meadows of the American Midlands. Brooks have not yet languished into July.

The bee hum of mid-June bids one look for yesterday and find it in the lush meadows. Butterfly wings lead one down the hillside with other Junes, a summer seeker without a real objective, the search itself sufficient. A dragonfly bids one to the water's edge, there to see mirrored the face of yesterday's summer vagabond. And all around, overhead, underfoot, in the very air, is the reminder, the remembering, the knowing and the very being of summer, the possession of it by the foreverness, the sweet foreverness of mid-June.

Then comes July.

I suspect that it wasn't wholly coincidence that the Declaration was proclaimed in early July, for in those days everybody lived closer to the land than today. And when a man has his footing in the soil he has little patience with outside interference, especially in July. He's too busy with natural problems to be very tolerant of man-made ones.

Corn begins to tassel out in July, and shoot up eight, ten, twelve feet tall. Hay, the second cutting, has to be taken in, and if it rains while the hay is down there's more trouble than a whole political convention can stir up. Store wet hay and you bid for a fire in your barn. Oats are ready to harvest in July, and wheat is ripening. A harvest too early finds the grain not properly filled, and a few days too late shatters the grain and loses half of it. Harvest time also happens to be hail time,

particularly in the West, and thunderstorm time everywhere; and even a high wind can level a field of ripe, heavy-headed grain.

Meanwhile, there are the daily chores, and there's the kitchen garden to tend. A countryman can't leave all the gardening to his wife, no matter how willing she is. She, too, has other things to do, what with the house and the canning and freezing for next winter and the daily cooking. But the garden is tended, for it too is a part of the independence.

The Declaration is a document for remembering. But there is another declaration, unwritten except on sweaty faces and in weary muscles, to be read by anyone who goes out beyond the suburbs and looks, in July. It says the same things as the written one, and it says them year after year where men and women work with the soil.

July is the year at high noon. It is festival and holiday, in cities and towns, and it is the Full Buck Moon, and fireflies, and the smell of sweet clover at evening in the country.

July is meadows frosted with daisies and roadsides snowdrifted with Queen Anne's lace. It is nighthawks in the evening sky, and fledgling robins on the grass, and half-grown rabbits eating lettuce in the garden. It is thunderstorms that jolt the hills, rain like silver threads hung from low, dark clouds.

July is a sultry afternoon when the very air seems taut, when the darkness of deep shadow falls across the valley like a palpable curtain. The cloud bank that was a mere line along the horizon a few hours ago has now risen to cover half the sky. The air is breathless. The leaves hang listless on the trees. A crow caws, just down the valley, and the sound echoes as in a huge, closed room. Not another bird utters a sound.

There is an ominous boiling in that mass of dark clouds. The first lightning flash shoots across it and makes the clouds look twice as black, twice as ominous. Half a minute later the crash of thunder comes rolling down the valley, bouncing from hilltop to hilltop. A few minutes later there is another flash, and now the thunder seems to shake Tom's Mountain itself. Another pause, then a flash and a roar of thunder that shakes the house, makes windows rattle.

A gust of wind comes down the valley, ruffling the river, sending a series of small waves scurrying downstream. The big maples shake, more a shiver than a shake, really. Then the deep, tense silence is resumed, until another flash of lightning is followed almost at once by a crash of thunder, too close for comfort. It must have struck, you think, on one of the ledges just up the mountain back of the house. You look, but see no sign of fire up there.

The darkness on the woods far up the mountain turns to gray even as you look for smoke or flames. The gray marches down the slopes. You hear the far-off rush of rain, the pelt and swish and the muted roar. But there still is not a sigh of wind down here in the valley. Since that one breathy gust that ruffled the river the air has been tautly calm. But on the mountainside the trees are swaying, and there is the rush of appoaching wind.

Then the rain comes down the river, a gray, steely curtain. The whole valley seems to shiver. Trees tremble, their leaves rustling and pattering. Then the rain strikes the house in a rush, drenches the porch, drenches you. And the whole river is leaping in spurts to meet the rain. It is impossible to tell which is river and which is rain, where the surface of the river begins.

The maples swish and roar. Their gray trunks turn black as the rain streams down them. The apple trees in the backyard shake and spatter little green apples on the grass like a showering of green hailstones.

Then, swiftly as the rain came, the darkness passes. The clouds begin to break up enough for the sun to stream through. It is a silvery world, the air laced with silver threads; it gleams and glistens as the rain still sheets down. Then the rift in the clouds closes, it is dark again, and another flash of lightning rips across the sky, its jarring thunder not far behind. But the violence of the storm has passed. It rains for another twenty minutes, such a downpour as we get only from one of these spectacular July thunderstorms. Then the clouds really break up and the sun comes

Seasons / 46

out and stays out. It is a clean world again, a dripping, gurgling world, the air cool and refreshing. The roadsides are young brooks. The brook itself has come alive again.

I put on my mud boots and go out to straighten up the sweet corn in the garden, firm the roots in the soil, and give the stalks a chance to mature those ears that have just begun to show silk.

That's the way it is in July.

But July is also horseweed grown rank in waste places, pigweed in the vegetable garden, milkweed and stinging nettle and forbidding thistle all coming to blossom. It is purslane and rough-leafed Gallinsoga, or German weed, in the lettuce bed. It is green beans by the peck, and bean beetles making lace of the leaves. It is squash flowers, and the hidden squash borer. It is tomatoes coming to fruit, grass-green yet, and the big, green, horned tomato worms fattening for the chrysalis from which will emerge the beautiful sphinx moth.

July is get-up-and-go, vacation time for the urbanite. It is the shore, the lake, the country, anywhere but home. It is hot afternoons and sultry nights and mornings when it is a joy just to be alive. It is cherry pie, and baby beets, well buttered, please. July is a picnic and a red canoe and a sunburned neck and nose and a softball game and ice tinkling in a tall glass. July is a blind date with summer, and you are going to be with her all through August.

And August? August is the year at early harvest. August is the taste of roasting ears and the dusty smell of field-corn pollen in the country air. It is tomatoes ripening, red and juicy, and the insistent shrilling of the harvest fly emphasizing the heat of midafternoon. It is zinnias in tropical blossom, and the dark stain of blackberry juice on your fingers.

In August, of all times, it seems to me, a man must keep his bearings and his sense of proportion. The old Romans knew this. That is why they designated this time as *Dies Canicularis,* or Dog Days, and warned that everyone must watch his step. Dogs went mad, snakes were blind and specially vicious, the night air was dangerous in the lowlands. Ah and woe! Do take care in Dog Days, in August!

They were right in principle but wrong in particulars. Some dogs have rabies in August, but also in July and September, and skunks, foxes, and various other animals share this horrible disease. Snakes shed their skins now, and molting snakes are at least partly blind. In that state they strike at anything that disturbs them, so rattlers, copperheads, and other venomous reptiles should be avoided. And the night air has its miasmic aspects, especially night air in the lowlands, where it often is alive with mosquitoes. And the mosquitoes of ancient Rome, even those of our own not too distant past, were agents of infection, particularly of fevers and malarial protozoa.

Had we inherited our folkways from

Egypt rather than from Rome, however, we probably would observe a Thanksgiving now, in August. And Canicula, the Dog Star of Rome, would be a harbinger of plenty rather than of sickness and disaster. In Egypt the Nile rose in flood about the time the Dog Star rose in conjunction with the sun, and the Nile's annual flood brought rich silt to Egypt's flood-plain fields and made them the continuing source of plenty. The Egyptians undoubtedly knew the mosquito sickness and mad dogs and blind asps, too, but they celebrated the time of the Nile's flood and thanked the Dog Star for his favors.

August is the flame of phlox in the dooryard and the silken petals of hollyhocks at the roadside, blooming now up at their very tips. It is summer squash by the bushel, and winter squash swelling in pregnancy beneath the parasol of trailing leaves. It always takes me back to the Southwest, to the conventionalized silver squash blossoms of Navaho jewelry. The Indians out there revered the squash as a primary symbol of fertility.

August is ripe oats in the field, ready for reaping. It is alfalfa coming to purple blossom, and the farmer hurrying to take his second cutting of alfalfa hay. It is a languid river lazying toward the distant ocean, and languid fish in its waters. It is a springhouse brook shrunken to a tepid trickle.

August is a few impatient asters trying to compete with late daisies, and the daisies beginning to look rather tired. It is the flash of black-eyed Susans with their van-Gogh-orange petals demanding attention. It is day lilies almost through blooming and looking frayed and outworn. It is a few sprays of goldenrod in the uncut fencerow by midmonth, and whole forgotten fields of goldenrod in bloom by the end of the month. We tend to forget that goldenrod is a late summer flower, not an autumn flower like the aster; it is through blooming and has gone to gray, fuzzy seed before the asters reach their peak. It once was gathered and used as a dye for the yarns of our pioneer weavers, providing a cheerful yellow for winter dresses that no doubt helped brighten the dark days of December and January. Now it is commonly called a weed and falsely accused of causing allergic distress that should usually be blamed on ragweed. Goldenrod's pollen is too heavy and too waxen to be airborne or unintentionally inhaled. It provides both tang and substance of a good deal of our late summer honey, which is why the bees are so busy in any patch of goldenrod.

August is chokecherries ripe, and flutters of jays and robins at them, chattering, scolding, quarreling over seedy fruit that is too puckery for any human use except in jelly. It is elderberries so heavy with juice their dark fruit heads are bowed like hunched old women in coarse purple shawls. It is chicory in bloom, a weed in field and garden that came from Europe as an herb for the cook and went wild. A flower for the sunny days, when it opens its blue, blue petals; but on cloudy days it sulks and refuses to reveal its face. Late in the season its flowers will fade to baby blue, but now it is as bright a blue as you will find in flowerdom. Just down my road there is a whole abandoned lot taken over by chicory, and every bright August day it is like a patch of clear sky, unsmogged, unclouded, rich with June or October, come down to live on the land. It makes me think of flax fields I used to see when I drove across the Dakotas in June, vast fields of flax-flower blue that blended with the sky on the hilltops.

August is a cow, her spring calf now forgotten, chewing a leisurely cud and switching at flies in the shade of a tired-leafed elm at the far side of the pasture.

August is grasshoppers, their wings rattling like loose rotors on decrepit helicopters when they fly. They seem to know that time runs out, and they hurry to complete a life cycle. It is grasshopper cousins, the katydids, come to maturity and starting to scratch the night. Some say first frost will come six weeks after the first katydid is heard. The reckoning is not far wrong, where I live, though I seriously doubt that the katydids have any influence on the weather. We hear katydids for the first time around August 10, most years, and we usually get our first frost around the time of the autumnal equinox, approximately six weeks later.

August is crickets, too, particularly tree crickets, the blonds of the tribe, which fiddle monotonously every evening.

It is field-cricket time too, and you hear their trilling any hot afternoon, so completely synchronized that as you drive along a rural road it seems that the same cricket accompanies you, fiddling the same monotonous note, for miles. August is the peak of insect choruses, day and night, so persistent that the ear soon ignores them and listens around their noises. But when the chorus ends, with the first hard frost, the quiet of the night will be so intense that the ear will waken the sleeper, wanting to know what happened.

August is grapes, still green and heavy in the vineyard, and the lacy leaf where the Japanese beetle feasted. It is wild grapes festooned on the trees at the riverbank, their lesser fruit equally green, their leaves less beetled—perhaps Japanese beetles are too tame in their tastes to relish the flavor of *Vitis riparia*, the wild grape that flourishes in my valley.

August is algae on the pond, and it is the fat browning-green thumbs of cattails in the swampy margin. It is joe-pye weed purpling into blossom, and it is vervain in full bloom, great lobelia lifting its unmistakable blue spike of blossom above the stream-bank grasses.

August is a hot but lazier sun, earlier to bed, later to rise, and edging steadily toward the south.

August is summer thinking about the color and cut of her October costume.

Some years September is a part of summer, as the makers of the almanac insist it should be, in large part. But that is asking a little too much. By August's end the leaves are tired and the chlorophyll has done its season's stint. The sumac says this, with its early flash of war paint. Look along any country road the last week in August and you will see that scarlet plume in a sumac clump, warning of the flame that will race through the October treetops and of that golden scuffle of leaves underfoot, crisp as the weather.

September is the interregnum, the interim. Summer, after all, is put on notice by the rasping of the katydids. The sun sets before seven o'clock, daylight saving time, for the first time since May, and with the first breath of dusk the katydids start. Frost will come. That is the sum of the message now written on the sound tape of the night, hard though it is to believe on a sultry September evening.

But no summer lasts forever, as the sad prophet said. Probably this is to be applauded. Certainly it is nothing about which to order mourning. Summer is achievement, and once the purpose is attained there is no more meaning in it. The abundance has been created. Life has been assured for another year, another beat in the eternal rhythm. And let's not think of it only in terms of human life, little as we have come to respect that. Life is life, and there is a millionfold more of it in other species than in our own human tribe. So the insect egg carries the germ of life to another summer. The ripe seed has patterned in it another summer's bud and leaf and fruiting. The tree has

added another ring of growth to its trunk. The root is strengthened. The miracle has been performed another time.

Life goes on, some form of life. We, each of us, have known many summers in one.

Small boyhood in the Midlands, the Missouri river's summer-steaming valley, nights so sweltering that everybody left his bed, went down to sleep on the living-room floor or the front porch, anywhere that some touch of night coolness might reach and soothe. Nights when you could actually hear the corn growing, popping its joints, shooting up another two or three inches between dusk and dawn. Days when barefoot boys prowled back yards for green apples, fished in the muddy Nemaha for catfish, dog-paddled in murky pasture ponds and called it swimming. Hot afternoons when we stretched blades of grass between our thumbs and blew shrill, monotonous paeans to the sun: plucked dandelions, blew their winged seeds off to far horizons, blew Pan-pipes on the hollow stems, made curls of those stems for childish clowning. Hot evenings when we chased fireflies, watched the moon rise, dreamed vast, improbable dreams of far places—dreams that, incredibly, came true.

Lakeside summers with damp-cool cottages that smelled of mildew. Summers with the blaze of July sun on white beach sand, the endless roll of surf, day after day, night after night, till time shall end; the hiss of wave-washed sand, the foreverness of the wind. The sleek run of a canoe through water, the feel of a sailboat's tiller, the tug of the sheet, the soothe of sailing out beyond the breakers. The beach bonfire, the clambake, the songs, the summer romance that withered and fell with the leaves. The clams, the crabs, the bluefish, the stripers, the lobster when you were lucky or your father was affluent.

The hot High Plains of my youth, the ripeness of bluestem grass in the draws in August, the ripe buckskin curing of buffalo grass on the uplands. The slow drift of great galleon-clouds across the blue infinity of the summer sky, the blessed benison of rain to ease the blistering heat of July and August, the earth-shaking crash of thunder, the comforting coolness of high-altitude evening. The soar of nighthawks, and their high-pitched *eek-eek* as they beat their wings; the flutter of big night moths at the giant prairie primroses that opened their petals at dusk; the September flights of ducks and geese, crowding the few ponds and waterholes for a day's rest before going on south, the geese gabbling their good-bye to summer.

August in the city, the heat-softened pavement underfoot, the stifling reflection of wall to wall across the streets like the blast from an open oven. The cool quiet of the big central library, so quiet you can hear the buzz of a hovering fly, the whisper of an intent reader across the long table from you. The faint touch of green coolness in the park, and the hot shade

beneath a tired elm whose leaves droop on listless stems; the splash of an outdoor fountain, its momentary breath of coolness. The sweat-hot cling of the shirt or blouse to your back, the hot breath of a passing bus, the summer smell of the subway, hot, sweaty, dusty, like an unwashed old human body. The evening sense of coolness beside the river, and the hot glare of neon light beyond, where there should be the comforting cool darkness of the open country.

We share an infinity of memories, you and I, and every summer brings them back to remember again.

May ends, and summer is all around us, the urgency of growth, the insistence of life, the fruitfulness, the abundance, the fullness and the overflowing. The juices of life throb and the heart of life beats with a pulse like the surge of the ocean's tides. Wherever there is root room there is grass, there are reeds, bushes, trees, moss, and lichen at the very least. Fungus spreads its insistent threads and lifts its pale caps overnight. In the marshland the primal soup simmers in the summer heat, and from it come crawling, ephemeral-winged creatures that outnumber the stars. Life.

Whence comes that boast that man possesses the earth? Summer gives it the lie every hour of the day. Life is the possessor, not man, an infinity of life that will outlast all winters, outlast even the boastful, blundering follies of mankind. Summer proves it, the glory, the achievement, beyond all human dreams or capabilities.

*A brown thrasher in a new-leafed oak tree
on a June morning, ready to tell the world,
"Wonderful, wonderful, summer is wonderful!"*

Summer...
A Portfolio

No one really needs a solstice to know when summer comes. It comes when wild roses bloom, when wild strawberries ripen, when robins bring off their first nestlings. Daisies begin to frost the meadow, and chokecherries come to sharp-tanged bloom in neglected fields and fencerows. Summer is that season when the new leaf's chlorophyll works overtime, when the egg becomes a caterpillar and then a bright-winged butterfly, when tadpoles shed their tails. Summer comes and there is no mistaking either time or meaning, for the sequences are now determined. Budding and blossoming must come to fruiting, sprouting and growth must achieve the seed. There is beginning and continuation and achievement, over and over and over, so that it becomes the continuity on so grand a scale that too often we miss the larger meaning, seeing only the details. For there is a rhythm that is greater than the day, greater than the season, greater than the year. It is the rhythm of ages, compressed into any summer.

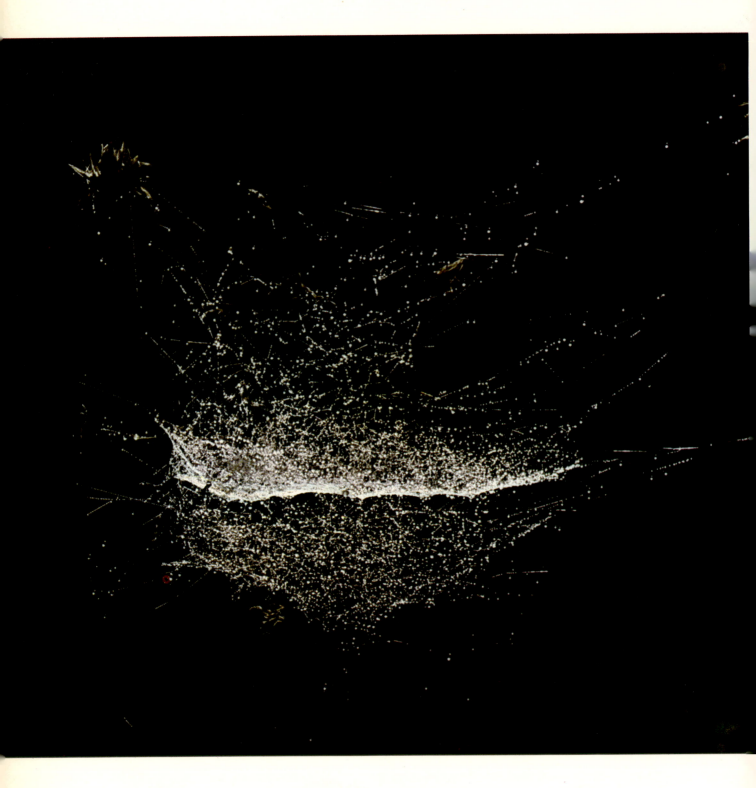

*Spiders are busy spinning webs in the grass, in the bushes, wherever
there is prey to be caught. Structures as simple as the orb web,
or as intricate as this bowl and doily web, made of silken strands
only a few millionths of an inch thick but stronger than steel.
Structures that are pure beauty when jeweled with morning dewdrops.*

A white-cedar branchlet shows the size of dewdrops on this leaf
of Solomon's seal. In some areas dewfall provides the equivalent
of 0.01 inch of rainfall in a night, and early morning mist gives
almost as much. Dew does not really "fall." It forms as condensed
moisture wherever the earth has cooled faster than the damp air.

The old herbalists used lilies
for snakebite, to heal wounds,
to remove "wrinkles of the face."
We cherish our lilies as jewels
of summer—the wood lily in a
field of hay-scented fern, the
orange-red Turk's-cap lily of
wet waysides, the Canada lily
with its nodding yellow bell.

Life probably originated in the Earth's tepid waters, came ashore,
plant and animal, in ancient wetlands. We go there today
to find such summer beauty as wild blue flag and swamp rose.

*We go to the really wet places, the bogs and the ponds, to find
the lovely little orchid called grass pink, or Calopogon,
and the bullhead lily, the familiar floating yellow water lily.*

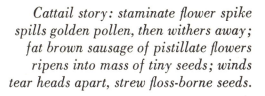

*Cattail story: staminate flower spike
spills golden pollen, then withers away;
fat brown sausage of pistillate flowers
ripens into mass of tiny seeds; winds
tear heads apart, strew floss-borne seeds.*

Colors of the summer sun
illuminate the meadow.
Gold, the massed gold of
hawkweed; the burnished
gold of black-eyed Susans;
the delicate, demure gold
of stargrass, cousin of the
daffodil; and the sun's
very rays captured by the
field's wild sunflowers.

And the colors of the summer sunset.
Orange, the massed nectar-rich orange
of butterfly-weed, of the milkweed family;
orange hawkweed, mirror of the sun itself;
spotted touch-me-not, with its bright pendent
jewel; and the orange "clover" of milkwort.

H. G. Wells, after watching a praying mantis a few minutes, said,
"I would as soon pet a snarling tiger as touch that insect."
Actually, the mantis is harmless except to other insects. It eats
midges, gnats, flies, bees, wasps, tree crickets, butterflies.
But when it turns its head and looks over its shoulder at you,
you wonder if this is summer on Earth or summer on an alien planet.

Autumn

Autumn is a recapitulation. It is the pale green milkweed stalk unfolding first leaves in May, the too-sweet blossoming early in July, the trapped bee and ant seeking nectar and losing life, the faded bloom, the swelling pod, the green leaf turned to gold, the pod fat and silvery and finally bursting like an ocean shell, the floss-borne seeds streaming away on the October wind, the empty pod, the stark stalk that will weather away and reveal its fibers for the nesting oriole in another May. That is autumn, bud to blossom, to seed, to leafless stalk and empty pod. That is the summation.

My first remembered autumn was in a grove of black walnut trees in the Nemaha valley of southeastern Nebraska. We had gone there on a Sunday afternoon to gather nuts, I perhaps four years old and riding on my father's shoulder, where I had the view of a man seven and a half feet tall. It was a crisp world, a world of rust-spotted walnut leaves, yellow as goldenrod, underfoot and drifting down. Of reddening red-oak leaves and brown-ing white-oak leaves and crimson swamp maple and still-green creekside willows. Squirrels raced. Scolding jays screamed that strangers were there. Cottontails startled even Father as they leaped from almost underfoot and sped toward the red-leafed, red-stemmed briar patches, white scuts flaunted. The sky was intensely blue, the creek burbled, the air was October-calm and mild as May. Asters and late-lingering goldenrod frothed and gilded the pasture edges.

We walked in the leaf scuffle and found the trees we sought, and Father said, "Not many left. I guess the squirrels got to them first." Then he laughed. "So we won't have to carry a sackful home, and you won't have to walk." And we went on, bareheaded to October, I seeing more of autumn from my high perch, remembering more, than a small boy's due.

October down along the creek only a few miles from where my grandfather brought a wife and the first four of a big family and spent the first autumn building a cabin of black-walnut logs on his homestead land. The creek where, in time, he built a gristmill and a blacksmith shop, and helped build the church and the courthouse.

He knew it, and I as the small boy helping look for walnuts knew it, thank God, before the farmers cut all the trees to widen their cornfields. Before they "channelized" the stream to put an end to spring floods in those "lower forties" and in the lower part of every town along the creek. They put an end to the floods, but they also put an end to the life of a stream that had watered and livened a rich valley ever since the Ice Age ended, ever since the first Indians came and made those Midlands their homeland.

Someone told me once that Indian Summer was so named because the Indians waited for those calm autumn days to make their worst assaults on the early settlers. It was, I was told, a dread term, a name for a time of fear. I wondered then and I still wonder if it couldn't have been the other way round, if it wasn't a time when settlers hungry for vengeance and eager to "clear the land" of earlier claimants made their own ruthless raids. Most of the Indians went on hunting expeditions in the autumn, to lay in meat for the hungry months ahead, and they took their women with them to do the heavy work, to butcher and cure the meat. The autumn hunt was a kind of tribal campout, a time of feasting and festivity. And if you look back at the records you will find a surprising number of vengeful mas-

sacres, of Indian women and children especially, occurred during those autumn hunts. If, indeed, the name Indian Summer has a bloody history, I am sure the whites did not neglect their part in it.

So, as I was saying, Father and I walked back up the valley with only a few walnuts in our sack but full of autumn ourselves, the mint-tanged fragrances, the leaf-smoke tang, of October. At one deep backwater of the creek, half a dozen teal took off with a flutter and a splash and showering of waterdrops that shot rainbow glints in the sunlight. At another backwater where we went quiet as a cat were two strange ducks, the most beautiful ducks I had ever seen. We watched, then backed away, still cat-quiet, and Father said, "Woodies! Prettiest ducks alive. I wouldn't shoot a woodie if I was starving."

Later there was autumn on the High Plains, where the Platte valley was almost clinking with the thick October leaf-gold of the cottonwoods. On the high flats to the south, between the Platte and the Arkansas, where the Cheyennes rode and took buffalo for winter meat, the age-old buffalo grass was curled tight with autumn ripeness, golden tan that glistened in the Indian Summer sunlight. Buffalo grass that had been there forever and, half buried in the thick-matted sod, buffalo skulls white as the valley mist at dawn, buffalo horns, short, thick, black, peeling horns, still there forty years after the hide hunters killed them off. The bones and skulls of the final thousands out of countless millions that flowed north and south with the seasons, like vast black waves of migrant life. Bones and horns of those incredible herds that darkened the tawny flats every autumn, knowing, even as the geese arrowing southward high overhead knew, that the blizzards were coming, that the hunger of winter would follow them like the wolves that pulled down the old and the ailing even as they plodded south.

Later, older, I followed autumn southward over those tawny flats, to the Oklahoma Panhandle and all the way to the mesquite thickets of Texas. The buffalo grass lay ripe on the flatlands, rippling like a rumpled rug, rimmed with the blue of vast distances. Ripeness, the short-grass country's standing hay that once fed the buffalo and the pronghorn, only God knows how many, and later fed the longhorn herds, bronze ripeness that would outlast the winter. That, with any sense of purpose and hope for a future, would outlast all the winters.

The memory, the recapitulation, of those broad, shallow ponds of March melt that the sky-darkening flocks of waterfowl welcomed as way stations on the flight north, the surging wave of green in April, those cool, blue cloud shadows of June and July, the blaze of August. I drove on and on, saw dusty-green acres of prickly pear, long slopes tufted with the broad green bayonets, the tall, dried flower stalks of soapweed yucca. And came to a hollow where a tall-towered windmill spun glints of sunlight, spurted cool water

into a broad, shallow, galvanized tank; and where the spill of water had eased the August sear stood a one-armed, wry-necked cottonwood as proudly gold-leafed as any tree along the Platte.

Another October we went westward with the sun, across the sycamored, hickoried, hard-mapled, soft-mapled, hackberried, slippery-elmed, willowed, sassafrassed Midlands, with swirling leaves at the roadside, shocked corn in the fields, pumpkins like full moons, the haze of leaf smoke and autumn itself in the air. Across the dusky plains. Past Denver and over the mountains, where the valleys were flowing with aspen gold, brighter than the dust that came down from Clear Creek in the sixties. The flanks of the mountains were maroon as old morocco leather where the scrub oak and the mountain huckleberries had a tenuous foothold among the rocks. The intense colors, the raw rocks, the porcelain sky, the creeks pied with their reflections where they were not white with their own surging haste. And on, down to the desert flatlands, where the sands themselves are autumn colors and spring is the blossoming after any month's rain. To the shaggy hills with their ripe-grass autumn, with their blue-berried junipers scattered as by the giant hand of a careless strewer of seeds. To the mesas where the squat, old-squaw piñons root in the gravelly soil and hoard their fat, oily nuts in tight, pitchy cones until they are gathered and dried in the autumn sun. Where desert folk, Anglo and Indian alike, go to harvest; where squirrels scarcely pause to scold at strangers as they reap and stow piñon nuts by the peck.

Still another autumn—October calls for wandering; it's the year's pandemic season for wanderlust—another autumn, in Idaho and Oregon and Washington, the far Northwest. Valleys of western larch, called buckskins there, turned the color of golden-tanned buckskin indeed, deciduous conifers, sometimes called tamarack, sometimes hackmatack. Wood that keeled the Vikings' longboats, when those Northmen were wandering the seas from Norway to Rome, from Britain to Iceland, to Greenland, to Vineland, which we now call Massachusetts. Reminders of those old hellions, of Eric and Leif and Karlsefni and all the others, there in the buckskin thickets of Idaho. And hills and flatlands of spruce and fir, dark and green and spar-slim. Then out of the woodlands and onto the plains and rugged grasslands again, still westward with autumn, with their willow-golden coulees, their balsam poplars, their aspens quivering in the hot afternoon. And asters, the ubiquitous asters, and late goldenrod, and late sunflowers. And on to the Olympics and the rain forests which hardly know autumn except as the days shorten and the nights get deeper and longer.

The many autumns of America, all of a piece and yet all different as the Alleghenies from the Rockies, as the Berkshires from the Sierras.

The many autumns I have known here in this corner of New England, where the laconic folk speak of "the color" when the maples put on their autumn finery. And here I must say something about that "color."

There is the temptation to plunge into a purple sea of adjectives to describe it, and there is the knowledge that such words fail utterly to do it justice. We say, "Was there ever such a year of color? I can't remember one." And we say the same thing next year, and the next. Reality, for once, outdoes memory.

It comes like spring returning with a new cargo of blazing color. Spring went north sixteen miles a day, and now autumn comes south at about the same pace, half as fast as a leisurely man might walk. Down through the rock maples of Vermont and New Hampshire, red and orange and gold; through the blueberry thickets on the worn-down old mountains, wine-red, blood-red. Down the valleys with their white ash turned yellow, their green ash turned blue, their black ash bronzed; with their willows stubbornly green till hard frost comes, and even after that; with their oaks like old Spanish leather, both in color and in texture of leaf. And the sumac, red and orange and fiery in-between, the flames that set the whole woodland ablaze. The lowlands shimmering with milkweed floss, the pastures aglow with goldfinches ragging out the ripe thistle heads, the boglands brown with cattail thumbs. And in the woodland openings, the meadow margins, now and then beside the highways, the come-and-go, find-me-if-you-can gentians, fringed and bottle, sky blue, cerulean, berylline, turquoise—and the adjectives prove themselves inadequate even now.

Gentians.

He had asked us to come to his island and see the gentians, and this day, he said, they were at their peak. So we went, and he met us at the dock. We drove half a mile through the woods, past the little swamp, and there on the lakeshore we saw them. It was a brilliant day, and there were hundreds, maybe even thousands, of gentians. Not quite the "blue cloud" on the grass that I have read about, but more than I had ever seen. I didn't try to count or even estimate. It was hopeless.

There were both kinds, the fringed beauties and the darker, closed bottle gentians. They grew in all kinds of soil, leaf mold, almost pure sand, even in gravel at the edge of the road, and they grew in shade as well as sun. Those in full sunlight were the widest open, but it seemed to me that those in the shade, and especially those that grew at the foot of the big white birches, were the tallest of all.

The fringed gentians were almost a perfect periwinkle color, as the artist knows and identifies color. The bottle gentians were very close to the artist's ultramarine. Most of them were, that is; there were a number of pure white ones too, albinos, and in their own way they were even more spectacular than the blue ones.

I was looking at one of the white bottle gentian plants, with a cluster of five blossoms, when a big bumblebee arrived. Remembering old discussions about how these blossoms are fertilized, I watched the bee with special interest. It climbed about one flower, looking for an opening, found none. It climbed on top, thrust a foot down between the tightly closed petals, got both front feet in, braced itself and pried. Slowly it forced the petals open, got its head inside. Squirming, pushing with the four hind legs, it thrust itself down and in. The petals closed tightly behind it. The big bumbler was gone completely, encased in that bottle gentian. The flower swayed as the bee moved around inside. I glanced at my watch. The bee was inside almost ten seconds. Then the petals parted slightly at the top. The bumblebee's head appeared, then its front legs, and it hauled itself out, seemed to catch its breath or at least rest for a moment, and flew away.

I watched the same thing happen at several blue bottles. Then I found another white one where a bumblebee had cut a slit in the petals near the calyx. It forced itself in through the slit, then came out. This was the only bee-cut side entrance I saw, though I have often seen bumblebees slit petunias near the base to get at the nectar sac.

Among the gentians were a good many of the creamy blossoms of Grass of Parnassus. Most of them were past their prime, but a few were freshly opened, and small bees were very busy at those flowers.

Close by, in the edge of the thicker woods, we found a number of lesser gentians commonly known as ague-weed, *Gentiana quinquefolia.* They are smaller than the fringed beauties, both in plant and in flower, and instead of daintily fringed petals they have toothed margins. Their color was a trace lighter than that of the fringed gentians.

How, we asked, did this gentian garden happen to be here? It wasn't a garden, of course, since it never had been cultivated, but that didn't really matter. It was just a relatively wild place with natural growth that the owner had kept somewhat in check. The gentians, he said, just came, to start with. There were a few of them, all three varieties. He cherished them, protected them, forbade anyone to pick a flower. When they came to seed, he gathered what seed he could and helped scatter it. Some of the seed grew. Gradually, with his help, the original plants spread.

I have heard it said that fringed gentians do not bloom till after hard frost. I can vouch that this is not true. Nor is it true that they open only in full sun. But as for their color, that never has been overrated.

The color.

Autumn is right now upon us. October, the very peak of that color. Enjoy it with me.

Just up the mountainside back of our house is one maple that must be among the loveliest trees in the world. It turns red, a special red that is full of glow and not in the slightest garish, a warm wine red, not as blatant as scarlet, not as dark as crimson. It turns that color all over, every leaf, each autumn. It is that color right now. I can see it the moment I turn the bend in the road, half a mile away.

There is a maple on the ridge near our lower property line that turns yellow, the sunniest yellow imaginable. It is on the very top of the ridge, where it stands out against the sky, and that tree, against that sky, the deep blue October sky—it takes my breath away. Magnificent.

There's a stand of white ash trees at the foot of the slope where Springhouse Brook comes down off the mountain and wanders across the pasture. Those ashes turn a splendid blue-green, then olive, then a strange yellow shade; or sometimes they go from the blue-green into a brown and almost-purple variation. Right now they are blue and bronze, old bronze.

Along the road in front of the house is the row of sugar maples. They usually turn yellow, golden yellow with sometimes a tinge of pink. The early sun comes through them as though it were shining through a golden curtain. At noontime they are lemon yellow. At evening they are still another, darker yellow. They are full of yellows right now, that incredible golden yellow. Before long the hard frost will come and loosen those leaves in the night, and half an hour after sunrise they will begin to fall like the first flakes of a golden snowstorm. The fall will increase as the sun rises and warms the air. By midmorning most of them will be on the ground, and the drifts of leaves there will reflect the light so that the whole roadside glows, even on the dark, glowering days of November.

Out beside the big barn, between barn and road, is one of the most beautiful maples I ever saw anywhere. It was a sapling not fifteen feet high twenty years ago. Now it is taller than that big barn, perhaps sixty feet high, and it has grown as a tree should grow, free of hindrance on any side, so it is like a huge egg set on end, symmetrical from every side. And each autumn it turns golden and pink and hotly orange, sometimes more of one color, sometimes more of another. Now it is like a fat candle flame in color and shape, perfection. What more need be said?

Thus it is here in our valley, in autumn, now and every autumn.

We think there must be more color elsewhere, so we get in the car and go looking. We go down the valley, or over the hill, or up the river, and it is different, and yet the same—the color, the flare and flame and sunlight in the maples, the dazzle of aspens and birches, the whole hillside, the whole valley, overwhelming with magnificence. From the hilltop there is a whole new panorama of color, colors you can't quite believe until you see them. We drive along the big wetland at the foot of the mountain on the far side of the valley, and that swamp is ablaze with soft maples; the whole mountainside beyond is a patchwork quilt of oak and maple and birch and ash in full color.

We go anywhere, and the color is all around us. We come home, and we remember the old fable of the house with the golden windows—right here, in our own valley, is the most beautiful place in the world.

It is the ripeness, the recapitulation, the summary. It is the red-ripe apple, the rosehaw red as the apple, the grape as purple as the adjectives of temptation. It is the harvest in woodland, pasture, meadow, field, and barn, in silo, pantry, and cold cellar. It is harvest on the mountain, in the canyon, on the dark, distant mesa, in the saguaro's desert.

You hear it in the night, the high distant gabble of the geese; you hear the geese in the day, that thin, penciled V far in the autumn sky, arrowing southward. You hear that four-note, six-note, eight-note call of the owls in the darkness. You hear the hoarse barking of the fox. And you feel the quiet where there was the insistence of the whippoorwill a month ago. You hear the frantic rasping of the cricket and the katydid, and the slow diminuendo as the coolness deepens into frost. You hear the echoing rally call of the flickers as they depart, the triumphant screaming of the blue jays repossessing the woodlots and the orchards, the hoarse chuckling and raucous laughter of the crows who really own the countryside by November.

You smell it, the ripeness, no longer May's greenness or the pollen of July's fecundation, or the dusty pod-and-hull days of August, but a smell of completion, of seeds matured and leaves crisped and juices no longer throbbing, no longer full of chlorophyll but not yet quieted into leaf mold. Ripeness, but not death.

You smell the frost just over the hill, just up the valley, in the night breeze, in the morning mist. You smell the woodsmoke from the hearth. You walk the lane at dusk and know the cidery tang of windfalls from the old apple trees, the winy essence of wild grapes where the 'possum gorges, the minty fragrance of wild bergamot and catnip and wild mint underfoot.

But always and forever, wherever you are, you see it. The color. The vivid, the lush, the subtle, the subdued, the countless tones and hues and shades of autumn in America. Leaf by leaf, blade by blade, from hilltop to valley, from dooryard to pasture—the color.

Even chemically it is a recapitulation, a consequence of what happened before. Not of frost. Hard frost dulls the color, kills it. Sunlight, rather, the day's length, the mysterious response of the tree, the bush, the herb, that we still cannot understand. The time comes, some signal probably from the sun, and the tree seals off its leaves, corks their veins after the last withdrawal of sugary sap. No more green chlorophyll can reach the leaves. The old chlorophyll bleaches away, revealing carotene and xanthophyll, yellow pigments that were there all summer, pigments that make carrots yellow and orange. Now they make the leaves yellow. And the sugars and starches left behind when the corking of the sap veins was done begin to oxidize into anthocyanins, red, blue, purple, that mark the soft maples, the dogwoods, the chokecherries, the gums, the oaks, so brilliantly.

Briefly, then, comes the celebration, the vast, marvelous spectacle that is autumn, to possess the land. It is more than the ripeness, more than the color, more than glorification of the tree, the bush, the vine —it is a many-faceted summary of the days, the weeks, the months.

It is the Harvest Moon, yes, but it is particularly the Hunter's Moon, the next moon after, the one in October.

Some customs die hard in some places. As coon-hunting, here.

Johnny came past that afternoon, said, "Big moon tonight, a fine time for a coon hunt." And I said, "Stop for me."

Darkness and moonrise, and he stopped and picked me up. There were three of us, Johnny and his son, Young John, and me, and there was Tic-Tac-Toe, his hound. A new dog. The old one died last winter, of old age and old injuries. Pooch, they called him.

We drove a mile down the road, to a friend's cornfield, and parked the car. We started through the corn, under that moon big as a county-fair balloon. Tic, the hound, sniffed the air and vanished in the shadows. Johnny told stories about old Pooch, who was a cat-killing mongrel condemned to death in a dog pound before Johnny heard about him.

"Any dog that kills cats," Johnny says, "will make a coon dog." So he got Pooch from the pound. "He was the best coon dog I ever had."

We walked across the field in the crisp moonlight. Tic yelped twice. Johnny listened, shook his head. "Rabbit," he said, and we moved over to another corn row. Twice Tic came back and looked questions at us and was sent out again.

"No coons here," Young John said. Johnny agreed.

We drove to another cornfield. Tic put up two rabbits, but no coons. Then we came back toward my place, and Tic took off across the middle pasture, up the mountainside. Johnny said, "Coon this time, coon for sure."

We followed. "Maybe," I said, "it's the old buck coon that has been down at the house, mooching in the compost."

Johnny was outlegging me, Young John outlegging both of us. Tic was bellowing in the woods on up, that coon obviously a runner. Finally even Young John was winded. We caught up with him and sat on a ledge and listened, watched the moonlight, were almost a part of autumn itself.

"I don't care if he trees that coon or not," Johnny said, half to himself. "Just being out here, with this moon, and hearing old Tic run—that's enough."

There was silence, and Young John got

to his feet. Then Tic began to yammer, a new note. "He's barking tree!" Johnny said. "Let's go!"

We found Tic dancing at the foot of a big maple that grows in a clump at the corner of an old stone fence, relic of the days of oxen and stone boats. There hasn't been a furrow turned on the mountain in sixty years, and the old fields are mostly white pines now, with the old maples in the fence corners, maples that set the mountainside ablaze in October.

Young John praised Tic and turned the big flashlight on the maple's upper branches. Far up, near the top, it picked out a dark shadow the size of a big buck coon. He held the light on it while Johnny loaded the .410 and debated a moment. Then he said, "Can't disappoint the dog," and he fired a shot. Bits of leaf and twig pattered down. Tic yelped frantically. Johnny reloaded and fired another shot, and that time he brought down the whole litter of a big crow's nest.

Johnny laughed, and young John probed the treetop with the flashlight beam. Tic stopped yelping, sniffed the bird-fouled twigs, and turned away. Johnny said, "Well, Tic, your coon got away. Must have gone down the fencerow while you were carrying on so." We found a soft rock in the moonlight and sat and smoked our pipes and told old stories about coons and coon dogs. Tic lay there beside us, tired and content.

Then we came back down the mountain and came on home. "Like I was saying a while ago," Johnny said, "it doesn't much matter whether we get a coon or not, a night like this."

There is a thread of leaf smoke and woodsmoke in the air, and the smell of frost. The leaves have drifted down, are skittering along the road. The goldenrod is a dry stem, a gray fluff of seed to be drifted away by the December wind, a few weeks hence. The Big Dipper is down on the horizon now, soon after dusk, and lines come back like the moonlight itself:

The Great Bear walks upon the earth
   tonight,
Come down to wash his paws in moon-
   lit lakes.
Across the moon is penciled the first flight
Of geese. . . .

And that "September Song," in which I tried to compress both love and autumn:

   Fox grapes ripen. Sumac fires
      (Love me, Love, and long
         remember)
   Torch the woodbine, scorch the
      briars
         (Starkissed, moonkissed, sweet
         September).

The gabbling geese, the barking fox, the hooting owl. And the Hunter's Moon:

Sun sets early and the Hunter's
   Moon
Bids man to follow the big buck
   coon . . .
For a man must go, and a woman's part
Is a half-warm bed and a given heart.

Autumn it is, harvest time, fall of the leaf. Or just plain "fall," when we speak the old Saxon tongue: "autumn" comes from old Rome, the old Latin, and it merely means to mature. But what matters the naming now? Even the months are mere Roman numbers by name, and misnumbered at that. Forget the naming, then, and indulge, participate.

You can talk about it till next April. You can sing its praises till your voice croaks and cracks. You can even try to whistle its airs. All you will achieve is words, words, words, with a note or two thrown in for variation. So forget such futilities. Summon your own summaries. Remember your own memories. Go walk with autumn. Hold autumn in your hand. Go out and watch autumn floating down the river, sailing through the air, skittering at the roadside. Know autumn in your eyes and ears and nostrils and on your tongue and in your bloodstream and your entire being. Here it is. Here we are. And here is the sentient remembering, the living part of the recapitulation of a season, of a year, of life itself.

*Autumn upstream sends a few bright banners
down the brook in greeting—red maple leaves,
a beech leaf, and the leaf of a slippery elm.*

Autumn...
A Portfolio

Autumn creeps in on moccasins silent as the glow of the Harvest Moon. Now the nights will have the touch and the smell of frosty air. Days will have the crisp-leaf rustle of fall as the reds and golds, browns and purples signal another year come to ripeness and to maturity. That is autumn's dominant note: maturity. Autumn brings a summing up of sweetness in the apple, of ripeness in the golden corn, of tartness in the wild grape. Spring was all eager reaching for the April sunlight. Summer was growth, and blossom, and August fruiting. Now comes ripeness, toward which bud and leaf and blossom all were aimed. The color creeps through the woodland. Cricket and katydid scratch frantically at the dark. The hoarding squirrel is busy in the oak. The drowsy woodchuck fattens for his long sleep. The barred owl's questions echo in the starry night. Autumn comes over the hills and down the valleys, in the smoky mists of Indian Summer, in the frost-crisp dawns of October. It is the power and the glory, to see and hear and taste and touch, to celebrate.

The spectacular beauty of autumn in North America is in its leaves,
which paint a horizon-wide landscape or glorify the least detail.
A flowering dogwood leaf dangles beneath next spring's bud,
a sumac leaf is caught on a thistle, a mountain maple leaf is lying
amidst the litter from other autumns, and the translucent red
of the sugar-maple leaf is captured by the bristles of a great burdock.

*The falling leaf of a hornbeam has
impaled itself on a twig. An old, old
stump, spotlighted by a shaft of late
afternoon sun, is decorated by the big
yellow leaf of a striped maple. A leaf
from a bigtooth aspen has fallen on a
lichen-covered boulder. And rusty fronds
of a bracken fern have interrupted the
plunge of the leaf from a white ash tree.*

*Autumn's royalty, clad in royal colors: fringed gentians
of the rare, elusive color and the sun-loving ways;
and those purple and gold spangles of fields and roadsides,
the big New England asters, surrounded by goldenrod.*

There are more than a hundred species of goldenrod in America.
Blooming from July into November, they are among the greater
glories of our spectacular autumns; and they provide a feast for
late insects—for bees and for butterflies like the monarch.

Thistles are a special treat.
The pollen-dusted bumblebee
and the spangled fritillary sip
at the purple flowers. Later,
the brilliant goldfinch rips
the ripe heads apart to reach
the sweet, ripe seeds, strewing
thistledown to the autumn wind.

Autumn's fruits are everywhere.
The Turkey oak's still-green
acorn hangs high in the leaves.
The bright scarlet bunchberries
gleam on the woodland floor.
The ink-dark pokeweed berries
dangle on their ruddy stems,
food for birds, not for man.

Fabulous milkweed, named for Asclepius, legendary Greek physician.
Its tufts of sweet summer bloom ripen into fat duckhead pods
packed with seed and silken floss. In October the pods split open,
and every breeze shimmers with milkweed floss as the brown seeds
are wafted off and away—if only to a dried-up wild-carrot head.

*Autumn comes to ripeness, in grass, in weed, in bush, in tree,
the time when tomorrow's green leaf is entrusted to the seed.
A season's work is almost complete, another beat in the rhythm
of the years. Now comes the time of rest, the recurrent pause
between the phrases of the eternal song, the green waves of life.*

Winter

Winter is the totaling of the year; and at the same time it is the summoning, the readying of the earth for the annual renewal. When I look out at the world after the first snowfall I always think of it as brand new, innocent and waiting for new and better transcriptions of the eternal and elusive truth. Not only is the litter of autumn hidden and purified, but the whole scene of man's argument and confusion is cleansed and briefly made immaculate. All things are possible again, even wisdom, even understanding.

Yes, I know winter is both time and change, time forever flowing, change forever varying. It is yesterday maturing into tomorrow. Even the autumn discard is the latent humus in which tomorrow's trees must sprout and grow. Winter is the dormant bud upon the bough, the ripe berry committed to the seed, the vanished insect to the fertile egg. It is the matrix for the miracle of spring, another beat in the rhythm of which we all partake.

It begins, of course, with the holidays. Most of us have forgotten that "holidays" once meant "holy days," and few remember that "holy" once meant "whole" and had a sense of completion. Holy days were holy because they were occasions for admitting that there are wonders beyond easy explanation. Then men undertook to rationalize those wonders and we achieved fragmentation instead of wholeness, as we so often do when we take wonders apart to get at their secrets. But we still had winter, a wonder in itself; and not even the impeccable calculations of solstice and equinox could alter one winter day or change the essence of the season. All the calculations achieved was a cold void of numbers.

The solstice itself once was an occasion for awe, when the ancients pleaded with the sun to refrain from vanishing into outer darkness. Year after year the prayers were answered. The sun did turn back from the abyss. But the wonder remained until we rationalized not only the solar system but the universe. Now we have worked ourselves so far out on the limb of rationality that our prayers, if any, are for our own survival. We are confident that the sun will turn back from the abyss, but we aren't at all sure what man will do next.

Winter has many dimensions, and unless one can stand on a hilltop or walk up a valley stripped to fundamentals, one misses some of them. Winter is more than a season bounded by a solstice and an equinox, more even than snowstorms and icebound lakes and wind roaring down from the Arctic tundra. It is primitive forces at work, cleansing and clarifying the earth. But it is also beautiful and awesome and full of wonder. And it rounds out the year, makes it whole. In human terms, it tends to take the edge off human arrogance at the same time that it makes the countryman proud of his own competence. In a sense, it makes the man who lives with winter whole again, too.

We like to think of winter as a season that begins around Christmas, though here in this corner of New England we are as like as not to be shoveling snow by Thanksgiving. One recent year we were buried under almost a foot and a half of snow on Thanksgiving Day. Then we didn't get enough snow to track a rabbit till after Christmas. The grandfathers who lived here a century ago "bustled" their houses with leaves in October to minimize the floor drafts of raw-edged weather that began in November, and they were wearing wool and nightcaps by Thanksgiving. Either the climate has changed or the race has toughened up, and I have

serious doubts about the toughening.

Despite the pious stories, I suspect that among the early celebrants of Thanksgiving Day were at least a few who were as grateful for frost and the end of the growing season as they were for a good harvest. There still were chores and outdoor tasks enough to fill their time if their consciences wouldn't let them loaf an hour or so, but the time of sweaty haste was past, and they were grateful for that. They weren't untried by winter; they knew what it was going to be like. But it did give a man time to sit and appreciate what he had earned. I know that up here in the hills, where memories are long and traditions are treasured, we have a tendency to stint our thanks and emphasize our own industry and foresight. We sacrifice the turkey, glorify the potato, the turnip, and the onion, and make pies of pumpkin and squash and a refined version of Indian pemmican that we call mincemeat. We eat our fill, appreciate the plenty; but we take credit for hard work well done. I have no doubt that this indicates a regrettable lack of piety, but it is really not an innovation. Man has always been, at heart, a glutton, a braggart, and a loafer when he could get away with it, and his prayers have more often been for mercy than to offer thanks. It takes the shadow of imminent disaster to get most of us down on our knees.

But by mid-December those of us who live close to the land are aware of such a shadow. The year approaches the climax of the eternal drama, the struggle between daylight and darkness. The ancient pagans built bonfires on the hilltops at the critical time and begged the gods to keep their little universe, a world they could span with their naked eyes, in order. We, sophisticated beyond such bonfire-superstition—ours are atomic fires, stolen from the sun itself—measure orbits and leave it to the astronomers and the physicists to keep things going properly. We even talk in terms of inevitability, in terms of another billion years or so; but we have to take that inevitability on faith, believing each year that winter is merely a pause, a time of summary and summoning, not the first stage of that long plunge into eternal darkness.

There always comes, for us, that day when we go up on the mountain to cut pasture cedars, as we call them, for fence posts. We won't be using those posts till April, but this is a slack time and too good a day to spend indoors. Anyway, a man can't just sit, even in winter. So we cut cedar posts, which is a kind of winter harvest as well as a good excuse to be up there on the mountain on a sunny winter day.

There are only a few inches of snow on the ground, but the two brooks we cross to reach the cedars are mere threads of black water between two shelves of white ice. The evergreen Christmas ferns hold green fronds up to the sun. Beneath the naked oaks are the mats of ground cedar and running pine, venerable ancestors of the white pines and hemlocks that seem to huddle in their groves. The sun is dazzling, with the snow underfoot, but so far off there in the southern quadrant of the sky that there isn't much heat from it. Our breath forms clouds of shimmery frost crystals around our heads.

We set to work in what seems a silent and deserted woodland, but before we have felled two cedars a crow flies over, cawing loudly. Then another. Blue jays hear the crows and come to perch in the leafless birches, pompous as fat aldermen, and criticize our work. Then the chickadees come, curious as cats, friendly as children, to twitter and peer and investigate each tree as it falls.

We fell and trim and pause for a breather, and I look out across the valley and think that if we didn't have winter we would have to invent it. The world is wider than a city block or a cornfield, and the sky is higher than a skyscraper or a silo, and a man needs a time and place to realize that. A man needs a hilltop and a winter sky, and the time to go there and look, and know.

We work till midafternoon, when the sun is down close to the horizon. As we go down the snowclad slope into the shadows of gathering dusk in the valley, it is so quiet I could have heard snowflakes nudging each other if there had been a snowfall. But it is usually a clear evening, clear and calm and the sky ice-green down at the horizon, as it so often is when a really cold night lies ahead, a night well below zero. But we have cut fence posts; we have seen the world again in its true dimensions.

There always comes that January day, too, when I do hear the swish of snowflakes as they fall, a whisper from the sky that comes with a gentle, feathery fall with little or no wind. Then I go out and catch a few flakes on the sleeve of a dark coat, and I marvel at the incredible intricacy and delicacy of each beautiful flake. No two are alike, though all follow the inflexible sixfold pattern or, rarely, a threefold pattern obviously derived from the basic six. I firmly believe that I could examine snowflakes all my life and never find two exactly alike. Far more industrious students of snowflakes than I am have looked and never seen identical twins among them.

And I think, looking at those flakes on my sleeve, that if I would comprehend the infinity of the universe, or even of life upon this earth, I would have to invent numbers to count the possible variations in a snowflake. I blow a warm breath on my sleeve and the snowflakes vanish, leaving a few droplets of moisture. It seems incredible that the sixfold snowflake crystal, evanescent as mist, could somehow be akin to the sixfold crystal of granite that has defied the erosion of the elements since the rocks first began to cool on this planet.

Sometimes the snow continues all day and through the night, and there is loose talk of "a blizzard," though the tempera-ture doesn't fall below 20 degrees above zero. Having grown up in blizzard country, I am tempted to scoff. This is a snow-storm, nothing more. A true blizzard would have ridden a gale in temperatures down to zero and below. A midwestern or western blizzard is winter at its most punishing. A winter of blizzards on the High Plains almost wiped out the range cattle industry in 1886–87; tens of thousands of cattle died, and a number of the big ranch outfits went bankrupt.

As a boy I knew blizzards, bitter cold, high wind, and driven snow that made the Colorado plains a bleak wilderness where even the jackrabbits burrowed into the snow to survive. One such winter storm that continued three days buried our sod-walled house to the eaves, and it took us two days to dig ourselves free. Today if I were trapped in such a storm, even safely under shelter with ample food and fuel, I could almost believe a new Ice Age had arrived and that there would be unbroken winter for the next twenty thousand years.

Our "blizzards" here in the Berkshires seldom last more than a day and a night, and a foot and a half of snow may fall. We seldom have more than that on the ground. It is, of course, clean snow and beautiful snow, as country snow almost always is. But the January snow doesn't last forever. By the third week of January we nearly always have a January thaw that sends the mercury up into the 50s, melts the deep drifts, sets the brooks to flowing, and makes us think of March, March mud and maybe spring peepers. Then the thaw ends, after two or three days, often with another snowstorm, and we come back from dreamland to cold reality. But for those few days winter has opened the door one wide crack and we have seen through, all the way to April. After that we can endure February. Even without the January thaw, we endure February, since there is no other way out of winter.

We enter winter, of course, sometime in November, regardless of what the almanac may say. As I was saying earlier, sometimes it is winter by Thanksgiving Day. Sometimes winter arrives with the November full moon, particularly when the moon reaches the full after the middle of the month. I must go along with one of the old beliefs—that the weather tends to change with the full moon. I have no clear reason for saying that beyond the fact that it so often does change, and sharply, at that time; but I do believe that the moon and its phases have a definite effect on our weather. Anything that can govern the tides in the earth's vast oceans, as the moon does, cannot be dismissed as inconsequential.

The Indians called the November full moon the Beaver Moon. They set store by the wisdom and providence of beavers, who by late November have their dams in good repair, their lodges snug, and their store of birch and poplar billets well anchored and accessible even when the ponds are deeply iced. The Beaver Moon,

then, is a time when man should look to his own lodge and larder and prepare for December's Cold Moon, January's Wolf Moon and the Hunger Moon of February.

In a sense, there is the summary of winter in the terms best known to those who lived with and on this land for centuries before the freebooters came from Europe in the fifteenth and sixteenth centuries— Beaver Moon, Cold Moon, Wolf Moon and Hunger Moon. Snug the shelter, build up the fire, feed the body and save the soul.

But there are other summaries.

The year sums up its seasons in dormant trees, in flown birds, in hibernating woodchucks and woolly bear caterpillars. It achieves a sleep, a rest, a time of quiet. Yet man, who is neither plant nor insect, neither bird nor frog, not even an animal that can slow his pulse and quiet his breathing in hibernation—man, whose blood can freeze almost as easily as water, survives. This, in a sense, is man's own summary. With less weather sense than a wild goose, with less stamina than a wolf, with less cunning than a fox, he still persists.

And he tries to achieve totals, out of sheer habit, for his own pride and the tax collector, and because he is that kind of creature. Totals of what? Well, for example:

I go out into the home pasture, booted and mufflered and my breath like steam from an old-time locomotive. I think I see a summary of life, at least a life process, in that halo of my own frosty breath. Then I am aware of the snow crunching beneath my feet, and it seems possible that there is a summary of snowflakes, of ice crystals that fell from a cloud a few days before. I go to the big rock we call the Resting Rock because we go there in summer to sit and rest, at peace with our intimate world. I find that the sun, weak as it is, has warmed the south side of the Resting Rock and melted the snow. The summary of flakes has vanished, oozed into the ground, leaving only a thin scum of ice. Then I look at the rock itself, a big boulder brought here maybe ten thousand years ago by the latest ice sheet. There is another summary, of basic substances and geologic forces. But again it is an incomplete summary, for it is a part of something far greater, now worn and shaped by ice and time.

Or I look out at the northern sky at evening, and out there toward the Pole Star and the Dipper and Cassiopeia is the flare and flicker of the Aurora, the Northern Lights. It must be the sum of something. I don't know what it's the summary of, unless maybe of winter days, or winter beauty. Or perhaps even of my own winter memories, for I first knew Northern Lights as a boy on the High Plains, and they were an awesome sight, filling the sky with that flutter of almost-light, then dying, then flaring again with flashes of red, of green, of incandescent yellow. On one long, lonely night ride I watched them for three hours, so brilliant at times that I

could make out the stitching on my saddle, almost count the hairs in my horse's mane, then dying down to a faint coal-glow red quiver on the horizon. I know what the astrophysicists say of them —that they are caused by sunspots and explosions on the face of the sun that bombard the earth with protons and electrons of hydrogen that are exploded, or perhaps fissioned, into oxygen, helium, nitrogen, and other common elements. But even now, knowing such an explanation, I cannot so easily dismiss them. That is almost like saying that snow is the response of water vapor to a layer of cold air, with no mention, even, of that marvelous six-pointed snowflake. I can summarize, reach a total, and to what end? The absurdity of simplification.

Or I go out on a January morning and find my river-valley world a glittering museum of hoarfrost, every imaginable shape of leaf and twig and dead stem encrusted with the most delicate ice crystals that frost creates. Tabular hoarfrost, like the pages of a half-opened book, miniature flakes of ice, to be literal, that fan out from a common binding. And everywhere I look, there is tabular frost, making such a twinkle and glitter and spectrum of prism colors that my eyes are dazzled. Or perhaps it is spicular frost, tiny spikes and points of ice instead of those flakes. And again it coats twig and leaf and stem with glint and glitter, the colors of the rainbow. And this? The summary, perhaps, of light? In the frost flakes, the frost points? Perhaps the sum of the night just past? All I know is that it happens, that it is an extremely beautiful part of winter, that it is ephemeral, since it vanishes in an hour of sunlight unless the temperature is down close to zero.

Or I go out in a daytime snowstorm and watch the wind, because then I can actually see the wind, see its shape and the patterns, the profiles it creates. I stand at the roadside and see how it sweeps down the road, swirling even as the currents in the river swirl around the rocks in summer. I go to the pasture and see how the wind curls the snow around a fence post, how it eddies around the dark stem of September's goldenrod. I watch the way it builds a drift behind each wayside stone. I follow it across the home pasture to the meandering brook and see the way it curls over the bank, graceful as a baby's curls. I see the spiral of flakes where the wind spins around the naked maple tree out beside the barn. The summary of the wind, of the storm as it moves across the land, as it came down my valley, freighted with that cargo of snowflakes.

When such a storm has ended I go out, the wind now stilled, and see a brand-new earth, its corners rounded, its harshness eased, its roughness smoothed. A brand-new countryside waits for a brand-new story to be written on it, a story never before lived, new as the snow itself. To see how nature abhors a straight line, turns the angle into a curve, soothes the eye, and gentles the landscape.

And when dusk comes again and the wind rises, now without a freight of snow but cold as Point Barrow, I stay indoors and know the virtues of a roof, a fire. That winter wind can howl like a running wolf, keen like a banshee. It can be cold as the midwinter moon, impersonal as the stars. Small wonder the woodchuck hibernates from it, the bear retires to its den and resents any awakening, and the deer huddle in the hemlock thickets. Even the hills seem to hunch themselves against it. And there is the total, all the summarizing necessary on a January evening.

I would remind you now how a snowstorm comes.

You know, if your senses are even half awake; you feel it in your bones, maybe, as I do. There are sun dogs beside the sun when it rises, those rainbow splashes of color in the sky with no connecting arch; and there are mare's tails streaming across the sky by afternoon. The next morning the sun comes up behind a veil of clouds that glow like the dying embers in a fireplace. By midmorning there is something unmistakable in the air, more than a hint, less than a sign. The sky is hazy. Not overcast, but filmed with a high haze that makes the sun glow like a white-hot silver dollar.

By noon the air is raw with a dampness that makes it penetrate, though the thermometer still stands in the mid-20s. It is so calm you can hear the flutter of the flocks of sparrows and juncos coming to the dooryard, to eat greedily at and under the feeders. Chickadees have been there all morning, too busy to stop and chirp a greeting. Small woodpeckers at the suet are so busy they don't even take turns, as usual, but eat side by side. Even the truculent jays can't bully the tree sparrows out of the feeders or more than momentarily crowd the juncos away from the spilled grain on the ground.

Now the haze thickens and shadows fade. Then there are no shadows at all and the sky has shrunken down till it hangs just above the hilltops. By 2:45 it is dusk-dim and there are spits of snow in the air. I can see it only when I look at the old gray barn or the dark pines on the hillside. But when I go out on the front porch to look at the thermometer I hear the snow, a kind of dry hiss on the crisp leaves that still cling to the black oak. It is just 28, a rise of 3 degrees since noon.

I go back inside and put on boots and a storm coat, and when I go out again the powdery snow is turning to flakes, big, fluffy flakes. A breath of a breeze has risen with the temperature change, and now I can see the flakes slanting down from the northeast. When I look up, all I can see is an infinity of flakes falling, no sky at all. The dusk-darkness has relaxed. There is a vague sense of brightness, as though the snowflakes were luminous.

I walk up the road, northward. The snow is wet and coming now in big, cottony clusters of flakes, the first stage of such a storm when pellets change to flakes

and there are so many flakes they clot and combine as though to make room to fall freely. The clustered flakes cling to my coat and some of them make audible splats as they strike the road. Then that phase passes and the snow comes as individual flakes.

The snow is still melting on the road, but out in the pasture it has begun to grizzle the grass. I walk half a mile up the road, then turn and start back, and it is like stepping from a dim hallway into a room with no shades at the windows. The wind I have been facing coated the far sides of the trees with that wet, sticky snow, trunk, branch, and twig. Even the roadside fence posts and the utility poles are white on the side I now face. I am in a world of fantastic whiteness, for the storm has etched a brand-new landscape in white, soft as moonlight, faintly aglow.

I turn back, come to the upper pasture and follow a cowpath, already a white ribbon through the grizzled grass, to the edge of the woodland. I follow another trail through the marginal hazel brush and up the hillside a little way. There I stand in a woodland that is all black and white, no longer stark but softened and elaborated. Trunks are whitened on one side, so the woods become a vista of tree trunks, each sharply defined. Branches are outlined in white and have become an intricate elaboration of curves.

I follow the trail, skirting the mountainside, for perhaps ten minutes, a path obviously a highway for the four-footed residents because in other storms I have seen there the prints of deer, fox, bobcat, raccoon, cottontail, snowshoe hare. The snow now is like a vast, shifting veil. Odd air currents twist among the trees, now and then catching a handful of flakes and swirling them back over a treetop. I have the feeling of walking through the bottom of a big, almost weightless, waterfall.

I come to a stand of white pines, and they look like gargantuan flower pots with fluffy white blossoms. As I stand among them, admiring, a twist of that swaggering wind catches the pine nearest me and shivers a whole crop of those big white flowers into my face and down my neck, a minor avalanche. I hurry down the hillside, back among the dependable hardwoods, down to the hazel brush with the pasture just beyond. As I stop to look across the valley two ruffed grouse fly from a briar tangle I have just skirted, silent as owls in flight. Somehow they knew they needn't startle me with that roaring takeoff. They fly up the hillside.

Now the pasture grass is almost white. The farmhouse and the outbuildings, two hundred yards away, are dim as though seen through gauze. The barn roof is snow-covered and blends into the background so completely that the barn seems to have no roof at all. The old apple trees in the backyard are inky black and ermine white, with fluffy cushions in every fork. The woods and hills beyond the house and across the river have vanished behind that curtain of shifting gauze. Dusk is falling and the world is shrinking to a countryman's personal dimensions. Another half hour and a man won't be able to see fifty yards.

I come down to the house, whose windows already are throwing their beams of light across the dooryard, light with the dazzle of flakes like countless meteors.

We go to sleep that night to the soft swish of light wind and blown snow, not enough wind to make the trees groan or creak. The temperature has dropped to 22 degrees. We waken to a morning sky still overcast but with signs of clearing. The snow has slackened. It stops soon after daylight after giving us perhaps twelve inches, though there was drifting and it is hard to measure. There is a two-foot drift in front of the garage doors. But the storm is over. Even without full sunlight there is a glow that makes me squint. It will clear before noon.

January and February are the darkest months, the coldest, the snowiest, in my part of the world. Now the rocks have lost the last of their autumn warmth and the earth itself heaves with frost. Now we climb the hardest part of that long, cold slope from December to April. Cold days and long nights are ours, the best and the worst of winter. Nights when the old star patterns in the sky gleam with the nearest thing to certainty and order we know, and one is tempted to climb to the nearest hilltop and touch a star with an outstretched hand. Late dawns, when the gray world comes slowly alive after darkness and cold that seemed eternally deep. High noons, with so distant a sun that only the faith of generations can believe it will be overhead again in June.

Winter, and its full moons.

Beaver Moon, when the wise countryman laid away his final harvest and made his shelter storm-tight. Wolf Moon, when hunger once drove the pack; when the long fang now belongs to the cold night. Hunger Moon, when the improvident and the unfortunate need help to survive; when the farmer calculated his wood and his hay, knowing his family would go cold and his cows hungry unless he still had half of what he laid by for the winter. And, finally, the first full moon of spring, full moon of peepers, of pussy willows, of sap flow in the sugar bush.

I cannot know the year complete or life complete without knowing winter. The year, like the land itself, demands that I participate, simply because I am alive. First principles are involved, to be ignored at one's peril. He who would be warm and fed in winter must know summer's sweat and muscle ache. The truth of cause and effect is written across every day and every winter hilltop. You are a part of the world. Your blood is a freight of hemoglobin in a stream of ocean brine, and the hemin is only an atom or two removed from the chlorophyll of the green leaf. Your pulse is as insistent as the rhythm of the days and the seasons, insistent as the ocean's tides. You are of the earth and the universe, and you cannot resign.

Last night, after a day of winter's cold, still magnificence, I went out into the dark of early evening to bring an armload of fireplace wood from the woodshed. I looked to the north and there beneath the Pole Star the Big Dipper lay close to the horizon, pointing the time of all time since stars were first patterned in night sky and man was here to wonder at them. The thin curl of a new moon was low in the west, almost down on the dark grove of pines on the mountain, a ridge of rock that was old when mankind was young. And somehow I knew that I was one with the wind and the stars and the earth itself. Winter was all around me, simple as the glittering breath from my lungs. I was a part of the mystery, the wonder and the awe, part of the holiness and the wholeness of life and the reason beyond all my reasoning.

*Last summer's wild bergamot stands knee-deep
and naked in the snow-buried meadow and casts only
a dim shadow where it once added a touch of lilac.*

Winter...
A Portfolio

Winter comes as a shimmer of hoarfrost, a mist of snowflakes from a scudding cloud, a roaring wind with a barbed-wire edge. It comes as a fragile film of ice needles on the pasture pond or woodland brook. It comes in the brittle cold silence of the night, the sun-dazzle or sullen overcast of day, echo of those ages when ice locked up the northern hemisphere 10,000 years at a time, reminder that the long cold and the deep ice can come again. Winter is the violence of storms howling down from the Pole, shrinking mercury into the bulb, blasting the Earth with driven snow, reshaping the whole landscape; it is driven sand and snow writing winter's unmistakable signature on the dunes of a Great Lake. And yet winter blankets the tender root and bulb, relaxes the fevered urgency of growth and fruition, brings rest and renewal, provides a time for summaries. It is the essential pause in the throbbing of the great, eternal rhythms of life.

Hard, white frost warns the deer
to move toward lowland shelter
before snow comes to trap them
in high mountain meadows.
The peaks already are white,
the aspen leaves have fallen,
the scrub oak's wine-red leaves
are rustling in a raw-edged wind.
Soon the streams will be iced,
the high meadows deep-drifted,
and winter's hunger will deepen
week by gut-pinching week.

*Night letters are written
in the fresh fall of snow:
"White-footed mouse was here,
ducked under the snow";
"Squirrel dug up acorn cache,
ate a morning snack"; "Rabbit
came this way, but didn't
pause to sniff ripe goldenrod."*

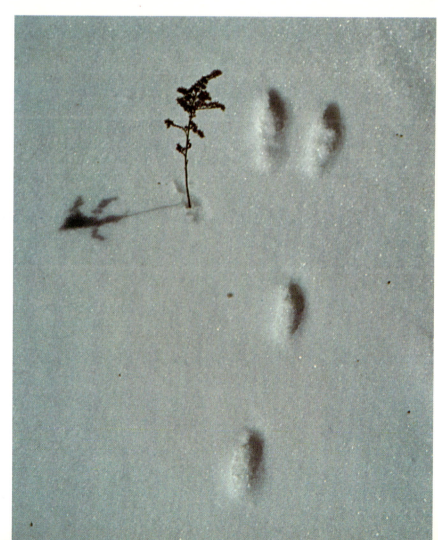

Ice seals the busy brook,
snow strengthens the seal,
but here and there the water,
looking black as polished jet
against the gleaming snow,
refuses to be imprisoned.

Beech leaves cling to the twigs, rustling in the winds
of winter till the sun summons the lance-tip buds
to prepare for their spring opening. Meanwhile, the sun
makes patterns on the snow with shadows of brown leaves,
a cold winter memory of last summer's cool green shade.

Wolf Moon, the Indians called it, and Hunger Moon. Full moon of winter, it looms in the night sky like burnished silver, but its light is as cold as Arctic ice. Haloed with the colors of sun dogs and northern lights, it overwhelms the stars and burns away the darkness, strewing the deep-drifted hills with charcoal shadows of winter trees in stark nakedness.

Photographic Postscript

The locations for *Seasons* ranged from a mountain meadow in the Sierra Nevada to a sphagnum bog on the shore of the Gulf of St. Lawrence, from the evergreen wilderness of Isle Royale National Park in the middle of Lake Superior to a streamside in the Cumberland hills of Kentucky, from a prairie in Kansas to a pasture behind Hal Borland's farmhouse on the Housatonic River in northwestern Connecticut, and many points in between.

The photographs were taken entirely with a Nikon F single-lens reflex camera. The lens most frequently chosen was the 55mm Micro-Nikkor, which is unsurpassed for closeup work. But I also used other Nikon optics—the 35mm wide-angle, telephotos of 105mm, 200mm, and 300mm focal lengths, and Nikon's remarkable new 80–200mm zoom lens. Some pictures, in addition, were taken with a 280mm Novoflex, using a bellows to isolate such wildflowers as the goldenrod and iris while preserving a strong suggestion of their environment.

All of the pictures were made in natural light, and all but one or two were taken with a hand-held camera at shutter speeds as slow as 1/15 second and as fast as 1/500. Exposures were carefully determined with a separate light meter, in most instances the Gossen Luna-Pro. My choice of film alternates between Kodachrome II and Ektachrome-X, depending on light conditions and subject matter; a very few photographs were made on High-Speed Ektachrome.

Pictures were taken at 20 degrees below zero on a January night and at 100 degrees above on a July afternoon, in gale-driven snow and in gently falling rain, on my belly in the soggy spring leaf mold and leaning precariously from a canoe in a muck-bottomed lake. It always was—and still is—a moment of expectation when the curtain of the shutter closed. And, later, when the yellow box came back from Kodak.

LES LINE

Dobbs Ferry, New York
1973